STEM
Through the Months

Spring Edition

by

Gary Carnow ■ Beverly Ellman ■ Joyce Koff

For information about Inventive Thinkers® and Clever Thinkers workshops write to:

Inventive Thinkers®
www.inventivethinkers.org
gary@inventivethinkers.org

Clever Thinkers
cleverthinkers@gmail.com

Some illustrations by Sian Bowman

ISBN-13: 978-1514176023
ISBN-10: 1514176025

Table of Contents

April

April – Poetry Month Lessons and Projects

April – Math Awareness Month Lessons and Projects

April Learning Standards

May

May – May Day Lessons and Projects

WELCOME

Welcome to *STEM Through the Months – Spring Edition, for Budding Scientists, Engineers, Mathematicians, Makers and Poets.* Designed for teachers and students, these activities help you make and create wonderful classroom experiences for the spring holidays. Using monthly themed events as a springboard, poetry as a language arts component and the maker movement for inspiration, your students will build cross-curricular connections as they explore STEM – science, technology, engineering and mathematics.

THIS SPRING EDITION IS DESIGNED FOR YOU

This edition was designed for teachers, students and parents as a companion to the other editions in this series. The activities are primarily for students in grades three through eight. We know you will find these engaging and innovative lessons and projects easy to adopt and adapt for learners of all ages. For each special or silly day of the spring months there is a STEM learning prompt. Need a lesson idea? Simply turn to the day of your choice and your off and running. The projects and poetry lessons have been classroom-tested and provide enjoyable learning experiences in a variety of environments: a traditional classroom, home schooling, after-school programs, scouting, gifted and talented programs, extracurricular clubs and ESL classes. For families looking for weekend or rainy day activities, we think you will find this to be a useful resource. And for kids who thumb through the special days and holidays, we ask, what will you make?

WHAT'S INSIDE?

Inside you will find STEM lessons, projects and poetry experiences inspired by holidays, special days, traditional observances and wacky celebrations. Drawing on the inner poet in every child and the "let me do-it-myself" nature inherent in all learners, the activities and lessons will help your students earn an "A" for the Arts and will bring STEAM to your STEM initiatives. Your budding scientists, mathematicians and engineers will practice creative and inventive thinking skills as they build knowledge throughout the year. Do not feel obliged to use these ideas and projects only around the spring holidays. The projects and activities are great with their calendar collaborations, but your curriculum and schedule may vary. We encourage you to use the activities and projects on a day that fits into your classroom plans.

HOW IS THE SPRING BOOK ORGANIZED?

We explore the monthly, weekly and movable holidays in March, April and May. Whether it's a silly celebration or a traditional holiday, you will find it listed here, ready to kick start the imaginations of your students. Next, Make and Do Days for STEM Learners, Makers and Poets highlight each holiday of the spring season with background information and STEM activity starters. Featured are four units of study that coincide with special days and holidays for each month. Each major lesson is followed by a poetry lesson that correlates with the unit of study. Students write poems in the style of the selected poet and learn about the poet in a biography that is easily duplicated along with the poem for use in your classroom. Additional poems that enhance the unit are also included.

Learning standards correlated to the Common Core in math, literature and writing are found at the end of each month. Correlations to the technology standards from the International Society for Technology in Education (ISTE) and to the Next Generation Science Standards (NGSS) in engineering and science, are included.

ABOUT STEM

STEM is an acronym for four disciplines: science, technology, engineering and mathematics. These four disciplines are related and overlap, but we tend not to think of STEM as unique unto itself. STEM has become "the next big thing" due to concerns that U.S. students are falling behind and will not be able to fill the void left by an aging workforce. As we become increasingly global dependent, we want our students to be on a level playing field. Educators and parents have no doubt heard the STEM acronym, but are often confused as to what it means or what it actually looks like.

As classrooms adopt STEM activities, teachers and students quickly realize that mathematics is at the core of all STEM disciplines. To be college and career ready, a firm foundation of mathematics is required. Science is also essential and is a part of modern life. Science includes a body of knowledge and the ability to follow methods and processes to construct understanding. There are many scientific disciplines taught in school (for example, life science, earth science, physical science) and they spiral and overlap. Important to the disciplines of science, engineers use scientific thinking to solve problems. K-12 engineering education has long been overlooked. The practical applications of engineering in conjunction with science and math foundations are a necessity. Technology is a part of our everyday life and should be a part of daily school practice. Technology, particularly computing technology, be it handheld devices or desktop computers is a tool that enhances learning. Technology can be an underlying support in all aspects of schooling, not just a tool for STEM disciplines.

As STEM education is adopted in the Common Core State Standards for mathematics and included in the Next Generation Science Standards (NGSS), schools are looking for innovative ways to integrate these highly engaging disciplines. We believe that STEM experiences are important for all students at all grade levels. We see STEM as more than just "real world" – we see it as high engagement and we know that you will find the projects and activities in this book helpful.

STEM GAINS AN "A" – STEAM

The national movement to provide STEM experiences for students gains steam on a daily basis. This is why we have focused heavily on the arts to integrate a big "A" into STEM. We know that you and your students will especially love the core poetry lessons. Students enjoy poetry and learning about famous poets and their poems integrate easily with your STEM and common core focus. From our teaching experience, we have learned that some teachers are uncomfortable teaching poetry. You will be amazed how easily these classroom-tested activities will assist young poets in discovering the joy of writing.

CONNECTION BETWEEN POETRY AND STEM

STEM learning and teaching encourages students to observe their world through their senses. Students construct knowledge through observation and practice in science, technology, engineering and math. This is also true for poetry. By exposure to poets, their lives and their works, students extend their observational skills as they write their own poems. And both poetry and mathematics contain patterns, rhythms and beats. Both are mysterious and need to be understood to comprehend. Then their secrets unfold.

WHY IS POETRY IMPORTANT?

Reading poetry out loud reveals a unique rhythm of sounds and beats and, in this way, poetry is immersive and experiential. Students are drawn instinctively to poetry because it allows them the freedom to use language in new and original ways. Students particularly enjoy straying from traditional grammar, capitalization and punctuation in some of their original works. Students are also intrigued by poetry that has an original visual look.

HOW STEM THROUGH THE MONTHS INCORPORATES POETRY

Each monthly chapter includes the work of four famous poets. Each selected poet is presented along with a biography, a sample poem and a teaching guide. Most of the poems we have selected are in the public domain. Those that are not are easily found. Your students will call upon their inner voices as they experience writing a poem in the style of the poet that they are studying.

Students will also gain an appreciation for the life circumstances and the period of time in which the poet lived and worked. Each poet is matched with a corresponding activity for each facet of STEM (science, technology, engineering and mathematics). The poets are the glue that binds each unit of study in the book and provide a unique language arts underpinning to STEM education.

TECHNOLOGY

We hope that you have access to some classroom or school technology. As technology using educators, we know that it enriches the classroom experience. For over thirty years, students and teachers have used technology tools to add exciting dimensions and high interest to classroom work. We have specifically designed these activities and projects to be enriched through the use of technology; however, it is not a pre-requisite. Paper, pencils and other common classroom supplies will suffice. If you have access to a few computers and a printer, great; we believe strongly in using what you have. There is no need to go out and buy the latest and greatest.

Many schools have employed Chromebooks for use in their classrooms. With a Chromebook, students use Google Docs, Sheets and Slides as their productivity applications. Students create their documents and presentations and store them in the cloud using Google Drive. Students can invite others to collaborate on their documents giving them the ability to edit, view and comment. You can also view a document's revision history and go back to previous versions. Google Docs plays well with Microsoft Word, OpenOffice, Pages and other word processing programs. Similarly, Google Sheets imports and converts from Excel and other spreadsheet file formats, including Numbers. Google Slides shares formats with PowerPoint and Keynote.

Many of the projects in this book use word processing, spreadsheet and presentation software. Whether you have access to computers with that software on the drive or Chromebooks with the application in the cloud, you are set to go. For classrooms with laptops or desktop computers with a hard drive, you have the additional functionality of editing video and using music software. Many tablets and iPads with apps like iMovie and Garage Band will also give you this functionality.

CLASSROOM PUBLISHING

STEM activities and projects come to life through the study and practice of language arts. The International Council of Teachers of English has identified five strands of language arts – reading, writing, speaking, listening and viewing (visual literacy). Students use language arts to show others their thinking, compositions and creativity. Making work "public" validates the work. As early as the one-room schoolhouse, teachers have displayed student writing and drawings. Work was sent home and no doubt "published" on refrigerator doors in the 1930s.

With appropriate technology your students can discover, invent and explore as they publish, illustrate and arrange their written work. These *STEM Through The Months* projects and lessons will be enhanced if you have access to word processing software or classroom publishing software. Your students will enrich their STEM content as they also develop skills in page layout, illustrations, color and typography. Students will also receive value from seeing their ideas "in print," whether they are working on a report or a classroom newsletter. We encourage you to explore the use of a simple digital handheld device, for example, a camera or a tablet, so that students can publish their work to digital lockers, websites or social media.

"STEM'ING" ACROSS THE CURRICULUM

You may be familiar with writing across the curriculum. Today we challenge you to use "STEM'ing" across the curriculum. The activities in this book follow monthly, weekly and daily celebrations across the academic spectrum, including English language arts, mathematics, science, social studies, fine arts, performing arts, and health. STEM learners work in a student-centered learning environment. Their participation is continuously encouraged through questioning, problem solving, collaboration and hands-on activities. Teacher facilitators guide students as they plan and design projects and work in groups to apply the rigors of science, technology, engineering and mathematics contents to achieve their goals.

COMPUTER PROGRAMMING

Now more than ever, schools are looking at ways to add programming into their curriculum. The tools to do so are readily available and even young children are learning to code. Most of the readily available block programming languages are related to Seymour Papert's Logo. Logo is more than just a programming language, it is also a philosophy of education. Logo employs discovery learning and is linked with constructivism, a learning theory. Constructivism relies on students experimenting and solving real-world problems. Students construct their knowledge and understanding through experiences and reflective thought.

A good place to get started is with Scratch, designed for kids at the MIT Media Lab. Scratch is browser-based and is on the web. There are millions of projects created and ready for you to explore, remix and customize to your liking. There are plenty of tutorials and educator websites for you to explore. Get started here at https://scratch.mit.edu/. Scratch works well with many of the projects in this book. In the Mother's Day unit, students make Scratch flowers. As you become familiar with Scratch, presentations and animations can be enhanced. Another similar program to enjoy is Turtle Art. Students can work with powerful mathematical concepts and create beautiful works of art. Get started at turtleart.org.

WHAT IS THE MAKER MOVEMENT?

The maker movement is a revolutionary global collaboration of people learning to solve problems with modern tools and technology. Children and adults are combining new technologies and timeless craft traditions to create exciting projects. The Maker and DIY (Do-It-Yourself) movements are fostering a new enthusiasm to work with your hands and see tangible results. In the 1990s, as we prepared a new generation of "knowledge workers," the goal was to round up all warm bodies and send them off to college, then to a cubicle in a career to fuel the information economy. This vision has not materialized. Now, more than ever, we need people who know how to do things – build houses, fix cars and solve problems.

As the Maker Movement continues to grow exponentially in local communities, makers in on-line spaces and physical spaces are coming together in meet-ups and hackerspaces to create, collaborate and share resources. Makerspaces are popping up in classrooms, libraries and storefronts. These spaces come in many shapes and sizes. A makerspace is not necessarily defined by what tools are contained in the space, but is perhaps better defined by what happens in the space – making.

MAKER TOOLS AND RESOURCES

Many of the lessons and projects in this book can be enhanced with maker tools and resources. The units and lesson extensions are starting points that can be enhanced with some of the exciting maker products now available. There are a variety of these low cost products that work with a computer and will challenge your students. A few to explore include:

- MaKey MaKey – http://www.makeymakey.com/
  MaKey MaKey is an invention kit. You turn everyday objects into touchpads and combine them with the Internet. The kit comes with an interface board, alligator clips, a USB cable and instructions. You can use any material that will conduct a bit of electricity to send your computer a keyboard or mouse input. Kids can become artists, engineers and designers as they create projects. They can devise games, mazes, musical instruments and much more.

- Makedo – https://mymakedo.com/
  Makedo are tools for cardboard construction. If you can dream it, you can build it. Makedo are simple plastic parts, a safe-saw, plastic "scrus" and straps that become joints or hinges. Using recycled cardboard you can build anything. Your projects will promote collaboration and problem solving.

- Hummingbird Robotics Kit – www.humingbirdkit.com
  The Hummingbird Robotics Kit enables robotic and engineering activities. It is aimed at ages 13 and up, but works well with ages 8 and up with adult supervision. The kit parts along with crafting materials can make robots, animatronics and kinetic sculptures. Hummingbirds play well with Scratch and other programming languages.

These are just a few of the many creative, open-ended products that your students can use to enhance your curriculum. There is a growing list of materials and kits chock full of creative projects to try. Do a Google search for maker materials and supplies and you will find a wealth of choices. A few examples include Make Magazine (www.makezine.com) and their online store MakerShed; the online store Adafruit (www.adafruit.com); Lego Robotics (http://www.lego.com/en-us/mindstorms/?domainredir=mindstorms.lego.com); and littleBits (http://littlebits.cc/).

3D PRINTING

In this book there are many projects where you could incorporate a 3D printer and use the products you make in some of the activities. Besides the obvious technology and engineering aspects of 3D printing, students can design and prototype projects in a way they could have never done before. Kids have made musical instruments, jewelry and scale models of buildings and monuments and so much more.

As home hobbyists have enthusiastically used 3D printers to make and create a variety of prototypes and products, now your students can, too. The cost of 3D printing has dramatically decreased and schools are beginning to purchase and use 3D printers. There are a variety of printers available and more are being introduced each year. Make magazine has reviews of these printers. Currently, printers for schools and for home use cost from $500 to $2500.

Kids are using computer-aided design programs to create files in the needed stereolithography file format known as .stl. These files are loaded into a 3D printer from your computer. The software that comes with the printer slice these files into layers. The printer begins the additive process of printing an object, layer by layer.

There are many websites where you can get 3D .stl files. Some of these sites feature open source files, which let you modify and customize the files to your liking. You can get an idea of what is available by visiting sites like YouMagine (www.youmagine.com) and Thingiverse (www.thingiverse.com).

NOW LET'S GET STARTED

We think you will find the lessons and projects wonderful additions to your curriculum. We know that *STEM Through the Months for Budding Scientists, Engineers, Mathematicians, Makers and Poets, Spring Edition* will jumpstart you to make, do and enjoy the spring season.

March Monthly Holidays

Adopt A Rescued Guinea Pig Month • American Red Cross Month • Employee Spirit Month • Expanding Girls' Horizons in Science and Engineering Month • Humorists Are Artists Month • International Ideas Month • Irish American Heritage Month • Mad for Plaid Month • Music in Our Schools Month • National Cheerleading Safety Month • National Craft Month • National Flour Month • National Frozen Food Month • National Hobby Month • National Kite Month • National Multiple Sclerosis Education and Awareness Month • National Noodle Month • National Nutrition Month • National Peanut Month • National Umbrella Month • National Women's History Month • Optimism Month • Play the Recorder Month • Poison Prevention Awareness Month • Social Work Month • Youth Art Month

March Weekly Holidays

First Week of March
American Camping Week • Help Someone See Week • National Aardvark Week • National Cheerleading Week • National Ghostwriters Week • National Write A Letter of Appreciation Week • National Consumer Protection Week • National Procrastination Week • National School Breakfast Week • National Volunteers of America Week • National Women's History Week • National Words Matter Week • Read an E-Book Week • Return the Borrowed Books Week • Save Your Vision Week • TV Turn-Off Week • Universal Human Beings Week

Second Week of March
American Camp Week • Bubble Gum Week • Children and Healthcare Week • Cycle Week • Fun Mail Week • Garden Book Week • Girl Scout Week • Music in Our Schools Week • National Professional Pet Sitter's Week • National Surveyor's Week • Newspaper in Education Week • Teen Tech Week

Third Week of March
American Chocolate Week • Brotherhood Week • Camp Fire Boys and Girls Week • Children & Hospitals Week • Health Information Professionals Week • National Agriculture Week • National Free Paper Week • National Manufacturing Week • National Poison Prevention Week • National Wildlife Week • National Yo-Yo and Skills Toys Days • Shakespeare Week • Termite Awareness Week • World Folktales and Fables Week • World Humanist Week

<u>Last Week of March</u>
American Crossword Puzzle Days (27-29) • Anonymous Giving
Week • Art Week • Brotherhood/Sisterhood Week • National Agricultural
Week • Meet Free Week • National Energy Education Week • National
Poison Prevention Week • Pediatric Nurse Practitioner Week • Root Canal
Awareness Week

March Moveable Holidays

Namesake Day ....first Sunday

Daughters' and Sons' Day ....first Sunday

Daylight Saving Begins...second Sunday

Casimir Pulaski Day ....first Monday

Fun Facts About Names Day..first Monday

Peace Corps Day ....first Tuesday

Read Across America Day................................. school day nearest March 2nd

Middle Name Pride Day .... first Friday

Employee Appreciation Day .... first Friday

Sock Monkey Day ....first Saturday

Girl Scout Sunday.....................................Sunday closest to March 12

Fill Our Staplers Day..................................... day after Daylight Saving begins

Registered Dietician Day ....second Wednesday

Popcorn Lover's Day .... second Thursday

International Fanny Pack Day ....second Saturday

National Urban Ballroom Dancing Day ....second Saturday

Absolutely Incredible Kid Day.. third Thursday

Corn Dog Day .... third Saturday

National Quilting Day.. third Saturday

American Diabetes Association Alert Day .... fourth Tuesday

Manatee Appreciation Day ....last Wednesday

March Days for STEM Makers and Poets

Day		Make and Do
1	Peanut Butter Lover's Day	Do you like smooth or crunchy? Perhaps you like your peanut butter laced with jam or chocolate. There are hundreds of kinds of peanut butter available and Americans on average eat three pounds a year. Create three word problems using some fun peanut butter facts. For example, it takes 540 peanuts to make a 12-ounce jar of peanut butter. Did you know that an acre of peanuts makes 30,000 peanut butter sandwiches?
2	Dr. Seuss Day	Dr. Seuss, Theodor Seuss Geisel, was born on this day in 1904. He wrote and illustrated over forty-five children's books, including The Cat in the Hat and Green Eggs and Ham. This day has been adopted as Read Across America Day in his honor. Start with your favorite Dr. Seuss book and create your own story in the style of Dr. Seuss. For example, rewrite the first few pages of Horton Hears a Who! or One Fish Two Fish Red Fish Blue Fish.
3	If Pets Had Thumbs Day	What would your pet do if he had opposable thumbs? Would he give you a thumbs up? Would she text her friends? Make a list of ten things your loveable pet might do. Draw a picture of your pet in action.
4	National Grammar Day	May the fourth be with you! Celebrate with the Punctuation Rap that you can find at http://www.nationalpunctuationday.com/playtimerap.html After reciting the rap, try writing a rap of your own about this special day.

5	The Hula Hoop Was Patented	The Hula Hoop was patented on this day in 1963. Arthur Melin and Richard Knerr, the founders of Wham-O, began making a plastic hoop similar to the wooden hoop that they saw Australian children use in gym class. The name Hula came from the Hawaiian dance. Twenty-five million Hula-Hoops were sold in the first four months of production in 1958. Hula-Hoop mania took off and Wham-O became a great success story. Find out why the company was called Wham-O and learn about its famous products including the Frisbee (first known as the Pluto Platter), the Water Wiggle, Silly String, Hacky Sack and Slip 'N' Slide. Create a sales brochure to advertise some of Wham-O's products. Include graphics and pictures in your brochure. Hold a Hula Hoop contest to find out who can Hula Hoop the longest with one hoop and with two hoops.
6	Dentist Day	Sink your teeth into this day in which we honor dentists and what they do for our overall health and well-being. How do you become a dentist? Do your research on-line and if possible, interview your own dentist.
7	National Cereal Day	John Kellogg and his brother Will accidently let some wheat go stale and found that it flaked when forced through rollers. The patent for flaked cereals soon followed. Their cereal was considered a 19th-century wonder food. Rice Krispies were their next big hit in 1928. What is your favorite breakfast cereal? Learn to read the nutritional information on the box. What is the healthiest cereal you can find in the cereal aisle.
8	National Proofreading Day	Celebrate National Proofreading Day by visiting the website for "The Great Typo Hunt" – two friends out to change the world one correction at a time < http://greattypohunt.com/>. Jeff Deck and Benjamin Herson traveled across the USA in 2008 to correct typos they found on public signs. They documented their trip, wrote a humorous book, and created the Typo Eradication Advancement League, known as TEAL. Do your part and photograph a public typo. Create a class picture album.

9	National Meatball Day	Who doesn't like meatballs? Spaghetti and meatballs, porcupines, Swedish or sweet and sour – there is a meatball for every taste. What is your favorite meatball? Find a recipe and create a recipe card.
10	Harriet Tubman Day	Honors the woman who led hundreds of slaves to freedom. You will find a wealth of information at www.harriettubman.com. Find out why she was a Civil War heroine. Create a Harriet Tubman crossword puzzle in her honor.
11	Paper was Invented in China	Paper was invented on this day in 105 AD. It was made from bamboo, fish nets, rags, and mulberry leaves. You can make your own recycled paper using a blender or egg beater; a 9" x 13" pan; a rolling pin; a piece of non-rusting screen in the size of the paper you want to make; two cups of hot water; and newsprint, scrap paper or wrapping paper. You can even add dried flowers or leaves. Get the complete instructions here: <http://dnr.wi.gov/org/caer/ce/eek/cool/paper.htm>
12	National Alfred Hitchcock Day	Alfred Hitchcock is well known for his suspenseful thriller movies that he wrote and directed including *Dial M for Murder, Rear Window, Vertigo, The Birds, The Man Who Knew Too Much, and North by Northwest,* among others. Have a Hitchcock movie screening party. Hitchcock appears in each of his films in a small cameo. Have fun watching one of his movies and see if you can find him.
13	Pluto is Discovered	On this day in 1930, Pluto was discovered as the ninth planet from the sun. At that time Pluto was considered the smallest planet in the solar system. Today, we know it as a dwarf planet. What is a dwarf planet? Why does it no longer qualify as a planet? Can you name the planets in order from the sun? Here is a mnemonic device to remember the order: My Very Excellent Mother Just Sent Us Nine Pizzas. Each word starts with a name of a planet (including Pluto). Write your own mnemonic sentence.

14	National Potato Chip Day	Cornelius Vanderbilt was staying at Saratoga Springs and he kept sending back his French fries. They were too thick. Chef George Crum sliced his potatoes as thin as possible as a joke, and the first potato chips were served. They also appeared in a cookbook in the United Kingdom in 1822. There are many science projects you can do with spuds. Have some fun learning how greasy your potato chips are at Science Buddies on the web at <http://www.sciencebuddies.org/science-fair projects/project_ideas/FoodSci_p048.shtml?from=Blog#summary>
15	National Everything You Think is Wrong Day	Today is a day to avoid beginning sentences with "I think" as you will probably be wrong. But don't fret, tomorrow will be here soon enough. For today, make a list of five things that you think are wrong.
16	National Panda Day	Giant pandas are black and white bears that live in the bamboo forests in central China. They are very rare and symbolize endangered species. There are less than 2,000 pandas in the wild and more than 300 pandas in zoos and breeding centers. Two giant pandas are at the National Zoo in Washington, D.C. and you can watch them on the web at <http://nationalzoo.si.edu/animals/webcams/giant-panda.cfm>. Research why pandas are endangered. Create a save the panda booklet with pertinent facts.
17	St. Patrick's Day	Finding a four-leaf clover is considered lucky because on average there is only one four-leaf clover for every 10,000 three-leaf clovers. Growing clover lawns are popular today because they look green and don't need a lot of water. Find a copy of The Old Farmer's Almanac or go online. Find out four benefits to growing clover. For younger children, plant clover shamrocks. Using small pots, fill with soil leaving ½ inch space and place five tiny shamrock seeds. Cover with a thin layer of soil. Water and cover with plastic wrap. Leave in a sunny location. Observe and discuss each day. The seeds will sprout in three to five days. Remove the plastic wrap. Wrap the pot with a festive green ribbon and send home on St. Patrick's Day.

18	Sloppy Joe Day	Sloppy Joe Sandwiches were first served in Havana, Cuba in the early 1900s, although some historians attribute the original Sloppy Joe to a café in Sioux City, Iowa. A cook named Joe added tomato sauce to ground beef and served his "loose meat" between bread. Today, Sloppy Joes continue to be a favorite in Iowa and in other parts of the Midwest. There is also a Sloppy Joe's Bar in Key West, Florida that opened on the day Prohibition was repealed. In 1969, Hunt's introduced the Manwich, a Sloppy Joe in a can. Find a recipe for Sloppy Joes, create a shopping list and make dinner for your family. Keep track of the cost of each item and determine how much it costs per serving. Use a spreadsheet to determine the amount of ingredients you would need to serve ten people, twenty-five people and one hundred people.
19	National Quilting Day	National Quilting Day is a great day to study the mathematics of tessellating shapes and applying transformational geometry in quilt patterns. Slide (translate), turn (rotate), and flip (reflect) quilt pieces to create a tessellating quilt. Start with a Quilt Square Challenge. Each student needs nine squares. Use a two-inch paper square and draw a diagonal line. Make half of the square black, leave the other half white. Starting with four squares, create as many patterns as possible on a four square grid. When proficient, do the same with all nine squares on a nine square grid. Try making quilts with unified color schemes like red, white and blue for patriotic quilts and black and orange for Halloween. When you are pleased with your design, paste it onto a separate piece of paper. Combine class tessellations into a larger bulletin board display.

20	World Storytelling Day	Each year on the March equinox, World Storytelling events take place around the globe. A theme is globally shared. Past themes have included Birds, Trees, Monsters and Dragons, Fortune and Fate, and Dreams. For 2016 the theme is Strong Women and for 2017 the theme is Transformation. Plan a storytelling festival. Develop a time schedule. Will your storytellers rotate or will your listeners move from area to area? Will you include an open mic "story swapping" event? Use a swatch of cloth as a ticket to the event. Use different patterns for storytellers and for guests. You may choose to use a distinct color or pattern to direct guests to a certain area of your festival venue. Give your storytellers a fixed amount of time, for example, three minutes. The presentations should be theatrical, interesting and well rehearsed.
21	National Fragrance Day	Today is National Fragrance Day and to celebrate have student groups learn about the sense of smell (olfaction). Prepare items with distinctive smells in separate plastic containers so as not to mix the smells. Blindfold student volunteers and have students identify the items by smell. Rate the smell as strong, pleasant or neutral; and jot down any memories associated with the smell. You only need small amounts of each item --- for example, lemon, cedar wood, orange peels, perfume soaked cotton, banana, pine needles, coffee, vanilla, dirt, onion, rose petals, saw dust, ginger, potato chips, pencil shavings, peppermint. After noses are proficient, make your own perfume. Place one cup of water in a bowl. Add a dash of vanilla flavoring, a dash of cinnamon and a few cloves. Let the mixture sit overnight and filter it with a coffee filter. Experiment by adding additional amounts of ingredients. What will you call your fragrance? Design a label for your fragrance bottle.

22	National Goof-Off Day	Today is a day to relax, unwind and do everything except what you are supposed to do. In other words, goof-off, assuming you won't get in trouble at school. If you can goof-off, what would you like to do? Would you play games, take a walk, read a book, or watch television? Perhaps you have other activities that would be fun. Create a survey to find out what people like to do when they goof-off. Does it change with age? Display your results in a pictorial graph.
23	United Nations World Meteorological Day	World Meteorological Day is a global observance dating back to 1873 and today is sponsored by the United Nations. In a group, create a feature report for the evening news. Perhaps you will compare the weather in different parts of the United States and determine how many hot days or snow days occurred. Or your group may wish to research historically how the weather in your region has changed in the last five years.
24	Chocolate Covered Raisin Day	Today is Chocolate Covered Raisin Day. You can make your own by melting ¼ cup dark chocolate chips and ½ tablespoon of coconut oil in the microwave for one minute. Stir well and add one and half cups of raisins. Pour the mixture onto parchment paper in a thin layer and freeze to firm. Break apart. Alternatively, you can buy ready-made Raisinets. If you eat ten pieces, you have consumed 41 calories. How many minutes of walking will it take you to burn off 41 calories? How many minutes of running? How many minutes of jumping rope?
25	Tolkien Reading Day	J.R.R. Tolkien's fantasy novel, *The Lord of the Rings*, includes the poem *All That is Gold Does Not Glitter*. The poem reads: *All that is gold does not glitter, / Not all those who wander are lost; / The old that is strong does not wither, / Deep roots are not reached by the frost. / From the ashes a fire shall be woken, / A light from the shadows shall spring; / Renewed shall be blade that was broken, / The crownless again shall be king.* What does Tolkien mean by "all that is gold does not glitter" and "not all who wander are lost?"

26	Make Up Your Own Holiday	Today is the day to make up your own holiday. What would you like to celebrate and why? What special customs are observed on this day? How do people celebrate your holiday? Create a symbol for your holiday and write a paragraph about your celebratory day.
27	Quirky Country Music Song Titles Day	Country music originated in the Southern United States in the 1920s. This genre has its roots in cowboy music of the west and folk music of the southeast. The vocals are simple in harmony and form and usually accompanied by guitars, violins, harmonicas and banjos. The titles of the songs can be funny and quirky, for example, *Mama Get the Hammer (There's A Fly on Daddy's Head)* and *I Sold a Car to a Guy Who Stole My Girl, But it Don't Run So We're Even.* Find 10 funny titles and make up three of your own. You can even hear and see some of these songs performed on YouTube.
28	Barnum and Bailey Day	The American Circus was a type of entertainment that made its way to America in the 1700s, starting as equestrian exhibitions, clown performances and exotic animal displays. The history of the American circus is fascinating to research and learn about. The Ringling Brother's Barnum and Bailey Circus has performed across the United States for over 145 years. Learn more about circus life by visiting http://www.pbs.org/opb/circus/in-the-ring/history-circus/ where you will find videos and historical information. If you were to plan your own circus, what would you name it? What acts would be part of your circus?
29	Smoke and Mirrors Day	Today we celebrate deceit, deception and the art of fraudulent cunning as well as all kinds of trickery and the art of distraction. The term "smoke and mirrors" means what we are looking at isn't necessarily what it appears to be. Magic tricks are illusions that often hide behind smoke and mirrors. Learn a card trick to celebrate today. You will find simple instructions on the Internet or on YouTube.

30	National Pencil Day	Hymen Lipman received a patent on this day in 1858 for attaching an eraser to a pencil. That is why today is National Pencil Day. Erasers were first invented by Edward Naime in 1770, but Lipman put the two together. Try one of these fun pencil activities. (1) Write a story from the point of view of a pencil. (2) Make your own pencil, you will find examples on YouTube. (3) Write ten things you can do with a pencil. Can you think of twenty? (4) Imagine that we didn't have pencils, what would your day be like?
31	Cesar Chavez Day	Cesar Chavez Day is a national commemorative holiday in the United States that celebrates the birth and legacy of a labor movement activist and civil rights leader. A model curriculum has been developed for grades K-12 and you can find it at http://www.chavezfoundation.org/. Create a technology-based presentation with words and pictures that demonstrate how Cesar Chavez educated the general public through nonviolent tactics about working conditions of farm workers.

Spring Lessons and Projects
Science Lesson: Invent An Insect
Poetry Lesson: The Caterpillar
by Robert Graves
Suddenly its spring! To celebrate spring, in the science unit, students will Invent An Insect and make a diorama. Technnology, Engineering and Math extensions expand spring learning activities. These lessons are good companions to the poetry of Robert Graves and additional spring poems to welcome the season.

Women's History Month Lessons and Projects
Technology Lesson: Wall of Fame
Poetry Lesson: Praised Be Diana's Fair and Harmless Light
by Sir Walter Raleigh
For Women's History Month we honor accomplished women with a commemorative postage stamp, Google Doodles and more. We study a poem which praises a powerful Roman goddess and a poem by Lord Byron who captures the beauty of a woman with his poetic words.

St. Patrick's Day Lessons and Projects
Engineering Lesson: Building a Leprechaun Trap
Poetry Lesson: Limericks
by Edward Lear
Just in time for St. Patrick's Day, we engineer a cardboard trap, make rainbows, and learn some "charming" math. And what would this day be like without Limericks? Poet Edward Lear gets us started.

Music in Our Schools Month Lessons and Projects
Math Lesson: Fractionated Rhythms
Poetry Lesson: The Violin – A Little Bit Nervous
by Vladimir Mayakovsky
For Music in Our Schools Month, we practice some fractionated rhythms, explore sound, graph musical glyphs and engineer musical instruments. Poet Mayakovsky brings an orchestra to life and three other poets bring us poems about music.

March – Spring Lessons and Projects

Science Lesson for Spring: Invent An Insect

As the weather warms and spring begins, thousands of species of insects and other small creatures around the globe become active. Each is adapted to survive a particular habitat. In this activity, students learn about the characteristics that identify insects and the various habitats in which they live. Students use their knowledge to create a habitat diorama and invent an insect to live in the diorama.

MATERIALS
- Small plastic containers
- Internet access and/or other research material
- Rectangular facial tissue boxes
- Watercolor and tempera paints
- Glue and tape
- Heavy construction paper
- Fishing line or string
- Scissors
- Assorted decorating supplies such as yarn, pebbles, twigs, tin foil, etc.
- Insect Diagram Worksheet
- Habitat Diorama Instructions Handout
- Invent an Insect Worksheet

PLAN
- Distribute the Insect Diagram Worksheet.
- Have students work with partners using search engines and other reference material to complete the handout.
- During a class discussion go over the worksheet to identify insect parts and what they do.
- Have students name some of the insects they have seen around school and identify the habitats in which they live.
- Have students go outside to search for insects.
- Distribute pencils and sketchpads.
- Have students sketch the insects and insect habitats they find.

DO

- Tell the students they are going to work in small groups to create a habitat diorama and invent an insect to live in the diorama.
- Divide the class into small groups.
- Distribute rectangular facial tissue boxes, watercolor and tempera paints, heavy construction paper, fishing line or string and scissors, as well as other decorating supplies to each group.
- Distribute the Habitat Diorama Instruction Handout and the Invent an Insect Worksheet to each group.
- Have the group decide on a habitat in which the insect they invent will live.
- Have the groups follow the diorama instructions to complete the habitat for their insect.
- When the diorama is complete, have the group members follow the rules below to invent their insect. The invented insects need to have:
    - the same body parts as a real insect (for example, it can't wear sneakers).
    - the same abilities as a real insect (for example, it can't drive a car or talk on a cell phone).
- Have each group present their insect and diorama and display them in the class.

Insect Diagram Worksheet

Draw lines and label the insect body parts of the fly on the diagram.

Abdomen .... Segmented body part that contains the heart, digestive system and reproductive organs

Antenna .... Sensory body parts for balance and smell

Compound Eye ..... Two of these with many hexagonal lenses that work together looking in all directions

Head .... Contains the brain and the eyes of the insect

Legs .... Six of these

Thorax .... Muscular part of the body section between the head and abdomen.

Habitat Diorama Instruction Handout

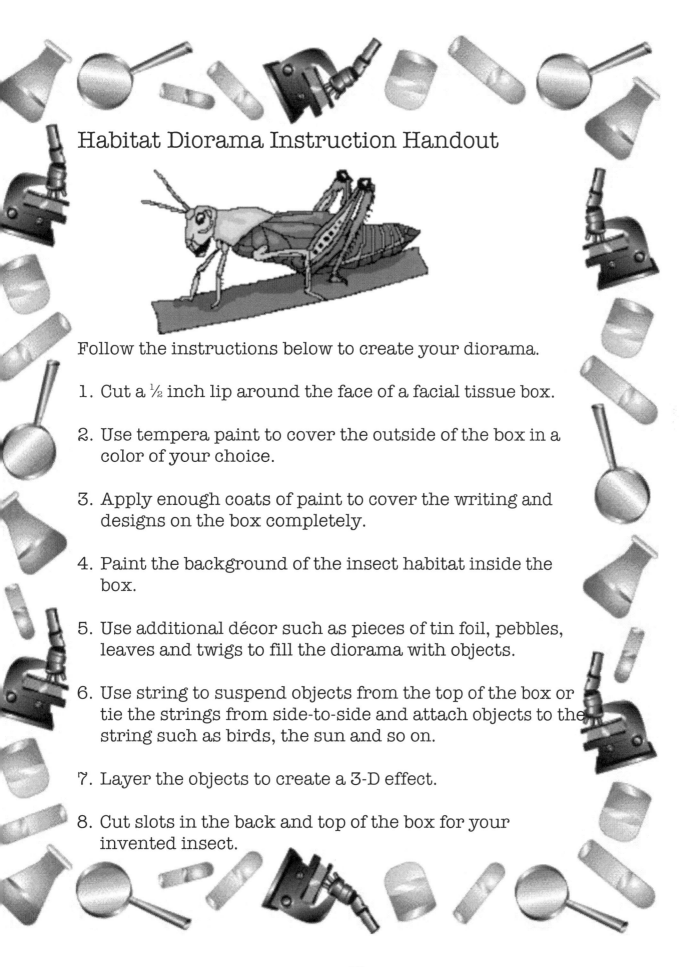

Follow the instructions below to create your diorama.

1. Cut a ½ inch lip around the face of a facial tissue box.

2. Use tempera paint to cover the outside of the box in a color of your choice.

3. Apply enough coats of paint to cover the writing and designs on the box completely.

4. Paint the background of the insect habitat inside the box.

5. Use additional décor such as pieces of tin foil, pebbles, leaves and twigs to fill the diorama with objects.

6. Use string to suspend objects from the top of the box or tie the strings from side-to-side and attach objects to the string such as birds, the sun and so on.

7. Layer the objects to create a 3-D effect.

8. Cut slots in the back and top of the box for your invented insect.

Invent an Insect Worksheet

Give the following facts about your invented insect:

Your insect's name _____

Its habitat_____

What it eats _____

Who eats it _____

How it moves_____

Sketch your insect here.

Create a cardboard version of the insect to place in the habitat diorama. Be sure to include all body parts. Attach a tab to the back of the insect and put the tab through the slit in the diorama to move it around.

Spring STEM Extensions

Technology Extension:
Vivaldi's Spring Awakening

Students listen to a selection of Vivaldi's *Four Seasons* and then work in pairs to create a musical spring slideshow. If possible, use one of the many YouTube presentations of the music with accompanying photographs as an example of a finished product. The following link shows how the music and pictures work together to make a delightful presentation.
https://www.youtube.com/watch?v=mFWQgxXM_b8

Have students work in pairs to create a digital slideshow of their own by incorporating the music to Vivaldi's *Spring Awakening* and pictures from the Internet. They can use one of their favorite slideshow software programs such as PowerPoint, Keynote or Google Slides, or they can spice things up and explore one of the free online software or video programs referred to below:

1. Prezi – https://prezi.com, a cloud-based slideshow program in which users create slideshows that zoom.
2. Glogster – http://edu.glogster.com/, a multimedia poster maker on which users' creations can be enjoyed on the iPhone, iPad, and iPod touch.
3. Animoto – http://animoto.com/ a cloud-based video creation service that produces video from photos, video clips, and music into video slideshows.

Below are some screens from the video created in Animoto.

Engineering Extension: Paper Bag Kites

Spring is kite-flying season. In spring, mild winds begin to blow away the cold air of winter warming up the ground temperature. As the ground temperature rises, the airflow rises and so do kites. In this activity, student engineers will begin by following directions to make and fly a simple paper bag kite. After observing how their kites perform, students work in groups to modify the directions for the original paper bag kite to design a new and hopefully better flying version. For example, they might try using a bigger bag or using a plastic bag instead of paper. They might change the streamers or the string or some other part of the design. When the groups have completed their new designs, they fly the new kites to test their modifications and re-modify as necessary.

Making Paper Bag Kites

To create simple paper bag kites, distribute a lunch-size paper bag, scissors, string, tape, crepe paper streamers, and crayons and markers. Display the following directions on a chart and instruct students to follow them without modifications.

1. Use crayons and markers to create a drawing or design on the bag.
2. Cut a very small hole (only large enough for the string to fit through) in the middle of the bag's bottom.
3. Wrap the string around a craft (popsicle) stick and place tape around to hold it in place.
4. Put the string through the hole starting from the inside of the bag with the stick remaining inside to stabilize the string.
5. Tape three or four crepe paper streamers to the open side of the bag.

Flying the Kites

When the kites are finished, go outside with the class and have students fly their kites while moving at different speeds. Bring the class inside and have a class discussion about what factors made the kite fly. Discuss how the natural wind or the wind created by running fast created a moving steam of air on the kite. Have the class think about the string and the streamers. Actually, a kite can fly without steamers, but it needs a kite runner to hold the string in order to both hold down the kite and to cause it to fly as it is pushed by wind.

Tinkering With the Kites

Divide the class into small groups. Make additional supplies available such as larger grocery bags, plastic bags, various strengths of string, rope and yarn, an assortment of streamer materials, hole punches and more. Have each group plan modifications to the basic paper bag kites they created. Have each group gather materials it needs and bring the new design to fruition. Go outside again and fly the newly designed kites. Conclude the lesson by having students write a paragraph describing the experience and what they learned about kite flying.

Math Extension:
Fractional Spring Words

Students will sharpen their fraction and problem solving skills by solving, creating and illustrating fractional puzzles based on spring words. As an example write the following fractional clues and have students solve for the spring-themed word. Note that each of these fractions represent the first part of the word.

1/2 of card + 1/3 of terminate + 1/2 of pillow + 3/4 of lard
Answer: caterpillar

1/3 of length + 1/2 of pretty + 2/5 of child + 1/3 of author + 1/6 of notice
Answer: leprechaun

Have students brainstorm a class list of spring words. Write them on the board or on a chart. Here are a few possibilities:

rainbow	butterfly	flowers	bunny	chicken	lamb
green	blossom	Easter	planting	insect	season

Divide the class into small groups. Students use pencil and paper to write as many fractional spring words and their fractional clues as they can in a defined amount of time, for example 20 minutes. After the set amount of time, each group shares its work with the rest of the class by writing a few of their best fractional spring words for their fellow classmates to solve. As a follow-up or homework, have each student write and illustrate their favorite spring fractional word.

1/5 WRITE + 3/4end TALK = WALK

Poetry Lesson for Spring:
The Caterpillar

Spring is the season when caterpillars transform from creepy and hairy insects to flying colorful butterflies. The caterpillar in the poem says he wants to remain a caterpillar whose only quest in life is to "eat, eat, eat." He knows that sometime in his future: "when I'm old, tired, melancholy, I'll build a leaf-green mausoleum" where I will "dream the ages away." He's heard that "worms win resurrection" and become butterflies, but to him this is not winning. He would still like to remain a caterpillar. In this lesson, students will become an insect that reminds them of spring and express how they think and feel.

MATERIALS
- Robert Graves Biography and excerpt from his poem *The Caterpillar*
- Word processing software, Google Docs or desktop publishing software

PLAN
- Read and discuss Robert Graves's biography and poem.
- Encourage responses to the following questions:
  - Where does the caterpillar live?
  - Who is "I" in the poem?
  - What does the caterpillar do all day long?
  - Why does he want to remain a caterpillar?
  - Why is he going to build a mausoleum and what happens in the masoleum?

DO
Getting Ready to Write
- Discuss the following questions with students.
  - What spring insect would they like to become?
  - Where does it live?
  - What does it look like? Encouraging detailed descriptions.
  - What does it do all day long?
- In the following questions, encourage personification as students answer.
  - What does the insect think about?
  - What does it think about its past, present and future?
  - What is it happy or sad about?

Writing the Poem
Tell students they are going to write a poem in which they become an insect.
Have students use page breaks so that their writing looks like a poem.
- Have students title their poem the name of their spring insect.
- Begin their poem describing where the insect lives and what it looks like just as Graves does. For example: *On a grassy leaf, crawling a short legged ant*
- Continue the poem becoming the spring insect. As in the poem, start with "I" and follow with what you are doing.

Editing and Publishing
- Students read and edit poems with partners.
- Have students draw their animal or insect and mount on a poster board with their poem.

Robert Graves Biography
July 24, 1895 – December 7, 1985

Robert Graves was born in Wimbledon, England in 1895. His father was a school inspector and published poet. His mother descended from nobility. He attended several schools before entering at age nine a very prominent private boarding school. He was bullied because of his seriousness, his outspokenness and his German name. To defend himself, he began boxing and became a school champion. He began writing poetry to express his troubles. His first poem was published in the school magazine in 1911.

When Germany invaded Belgium in 1914, Graves was 19 and he joined the British Army to fight in World War I. Two years after joining the army, he was badly wounded and was expected to die. He suffered from shell shock "and I couldn't face the sound of heavy shelling now; the noise of a car back-firing would send me flat on my face, or running for cover." The army accidently told his parents that their son was killed. He read his own obituary in the London Times.

Still feeling the need to defend his country, Graves returned to the army after his wounds healed. He spent a brief time in France and the remainder of the war in England. During this time he had two books of poems published and developed the reputation as a war poet.

In January 1918, at the age of 22, he began teaching at Oxford and married Nancy Nicholson. They had four children together. In 1926 he moved to Egypt where he taught at Cairo University. The following year he traveled back to England. Upon returning, he and his wife divorced. Eventually he moved to the Spanish Island of Majorca and became a full-time writer. By then, Graves had published many books of poetry. But poetry could not support him so he began to write historical novels, the most successful of which was *I Claudius*. It became an internationally famous BBC television series.

In 1936 he had to leave Spain because of the onset of the Spanish Civil War. He moved to London where he met Beryl Hodge who would become his second wife and with whom he would have another four children. They moved to the quiet English village of Devon. In 1939, war with Germany was declared. By the end of the war, Graves was ready to move back to Majorca where he and Beryl would spend the rest of their lives together.

Graves received the Queen's Gold Medal for Poetry. He was also one of sixteen Great War poets commemorated on a stone in the Poets' Corner in Westminster Abbey. During his lifetime he published more than 140 books, which included 55 books of poetry, 15 novels, 10 translations, and 40 works of nonfiction, autobiographies, and literary essays. His greatest love was poetry.

The Caterpillar
by Robert Graves

In his poem *The Caterpillar*, Robert Graves gives a new perspective on a caterpillar's life through the use of personification and a great imagination. He begins his poem establishing where the caterpillar spends most of his time: "Under this loop of honeysuckle." Graves describes what the caterpillar looks like: "A creeping, coloured caterpillar." He continues the poem, becoming the caterpillar "I gnaw the fresh green hawthorn spray." Throughout the poem, he writes about the caterpillar's love of his life and his reason for living: "I eat and swallow and eat again."

The caterpillar begins to think that, although he does not want to change, he must become a butterfly. He makes plans to build himself a cocoon which he refers to as a mausoleum. He writes that some say worms "win resurrection" by dying and becoming butterflies. But to this caterpillar the word "win" does not have a positive connotation because he would like to remain "A hungry, hairy caterpillar," and "crawl on my high and swinging seat, / And eat, eat, eat – as one ought to eat."

The entire poem is available online. You can search for it or go to the following website to find the poem. Copy, print and share the poem with your class.

http://www.poets.org/viewmedia.php/prmMID/20235

Additional Poems for Spring

In the poem *Spring Carol* by Robert Louis Stevenson, the poet describes the sounds of spring. Play the first movement of Antonio Vivaldi's musical composition *The Four Seasons*. How are the words of Robert Louis Stevenson similar to the music of Antonio Vivaldi?

Spring Carol
by Robert Louis Stevenson

When loud by landside streamlets gush
And clear in the greenwood quires the thrush
With sun on the meadows
And songs in the shadows
Comes again to me
The gift of the tongues of the lea,
The gift of the tongues of meadows.

Straightway my olden heart returns
And dances with the dancing burns;
It sings with the sparrows;
To the rain and the (grimy) barrows
Sings my heart aloud
To the silver-bellied cloud,
To the silver rainy arrows.

It bears the song of the skylark down,
And it hears the singing of the town;
And youth on the highways
And lovers in byways
Follows and sees:
And hearkens the song of the leas
And sings the songs of the highways.

So when the earth is alive with gods,
And the lusty ploughman breaks the sod,
And the grass sings in the meadows,
And the flowers smile in the shadows,
Sits my heart at ease,
Hearing the song of the leas,
Singing the songs of the meadows.

Much of Robert Burns' poem *Song Composed in Spring* is written in a Scottish dialect. Have students read his poem first and research the meanings of the words. Then write a spring poem using some of the words they have learned.

Song Composed in Spring
by Robert Burns

Again rejoicing Nature sees
Her robe assume its vernal hues:
Her leafy locks wave in the breeze,
All freshly steep'd in morning dews.

Chorus. – And maun I still on Menie doat,
And bear the scorn that's in her e'e?
For it's jet, jet black, an' it's like a hawk,
An' it winna let a body be.

In vain to me the cowslips blaw,
In vain to me the vi'lets spring;
In vain to me in glen or shaw,
The mavis and the lintwhite sing.
And maun I still, &c.

The merry ploughboy cheers his team,
Wi' joy the tentie seedsman stalks;
But life to me's a weary dream,
A dream of ane that never wauks.
And maun I still, &c.

The wanton coot the water skims,
Amang the reeds the ducklings cry,
The stately swan majestic swims,
And ev'ry thing is blest but I.
And maun I still, &c.

The sheep-herd steeks his faulding slap,
And o'er the moorlands whistles shill:
Wi' wild, unequal, wand'ring step,
I meet him on the dewy hill.
And maun I still, &c.
And when the lark, 'tween light and dark,

Blythe waukens by the daisy's side,
And mounts and sings on flittering wings,
A woe-worn ghaist I hameward glide.
And maun I still, &c.

Come winter, with thine angry howl,
And raging, bend the naked tree;
Thy gloom will soothe my cheerless soul,
When nature all is sad like me!
And maun I still, &c.

William Blake's *To Spring* speaks to the season through personification. Have students read the poem and write a poem where they welcome spring and ask it to perform its healing qualities on nature.

To Spring
by William Blake

O thou with dewy locks, who lookest down
Through the clear windows of the morning, turn
Thine angel eyes upon our western isle,
Which in full choir hails thy approach, O Spring!

The hills tell one another, and the listening
Valleys hear; all our longing eyes are turn'd
Up to thy bright pavilions: issue forth
And let thy holy feet visit our clime!

Come o'er the eastern hills, and let our winds
Kiss thy perfumèd garments; let us taste
Thy morn and evening breath; scatter thy pearls
Upon our lovesick land that mourns for thee.

O deck her forth with thy fair fingers; pour
Thy soft kisses on her bosom; and put
Thy golden crown upon her languish'd head,
Whose modest tresses are bound up for thee.

March – Women's History Month Lessons and Projects

Techology Lesson: Wall of Fame

In honor of Women's History Month students work in pairs to select and nominate a famous woman to be commemorated on a United States postage stamp. Students search the Internet to find biographical information including greatest accomplishments and other pertinent facts that qualify her to be considered for the honor. Students use word processing software to write letters to submit a woman's name for consideration to the Citizens' Stamp Advisory Committee, appointed by the Postmaster General. The committee reviews all proposals and decides which will be made into stamps. The Postmaster General makes the final decision.

Create a classroom bulletin board titled "Women's Wall of Fame." Students make two copies of their nomination letters, one to mail and one to place on the bulletin board. Encourage students to use a draw/paint program to illustrate their stamp for the display. Also, post any replies that your students receive from the Advisory Committee.

MATERIALS
- Computer
- Printer
- Internet access
- Stamps and envelopes
- Draw/paint software
- Word processing software
- Construction paper
- Glue, tape, other mounting materials
- Scissors
- Stamp Proposal Letter Handout

PLAN
- Students work in pairs to write a letter nominating a noteworthy woman to be commemorated on a United States postage stamp. In addition, student pairs will create a stamp of their own along with their letter to be placed on a classroom Women's Wall of Fame bulletin board.
- Write the following categories on a board or chart:
  - History
  - Science
  - Technology
  - Art

- ▪ Education
- ▪ Sports
- ▪ Other
- ▪ Ask students to name women in the categories listed on the board or chart that they think belong on the wall. Write the nominated names in the appropriate category.

DO

- ▪ Divide the class into pairs.
- ▪ Student pairs do an Internet check of women on the list that have already had a postage stamp issued in their honor in order to select a new honoree.
- ▪ Have each pair select a woman to honor.
- ▪ Distribute the Stamp Proposal Letter Handout and envelopes.
- ▪ Have students use the worksheet to plan their letters.
- ▪ Instruct them to use a word processing program to write and edit their letters.
- ▪ Students print two copies of the letter, one for the Citizens' Stamp Advisory Committee and one for the class Women's Wall of Fame bulletin board.
- ▪ Have students place one copy of their letters in envelopes and address them to the Citizens' Stamp Advisory Committee.
- ▪ Have students open a draw/paint program and use all of its functions to create their stamp.
- ▪ Tell students to include images, words and graphics on the stamp. For example, a stamp honoring Astronaut Sally Ride might use a series of graphics to create a space border, a student created picture of a space ship, and a caption such as "Sally Ride, First Woman Astronaut."
- ▪ Print the finished stamps and mount them with a copy of the letters on construction paper.
- ▪ Place them on a bulletin board to create a Women's History Month Wall of Fame.

Stamp Proposal Letter Handout

You are going to write a letter to the Citizens' Stamp Advisory Committee to submit the name of the famous American woman you selected to recommend for a future stamp issue. The Committee will analyze your submission according to standards that include a far-reaching public interest and inspirational content. Use the form below as a model for your letter and the content suggestions for the body of the letter. Compose your letter in a word processing program.

Letter Format and Directions

Heading
The names of both partners
Classroom and grade level
School Address
City, State Zip

Date

Inside Address
Citizens' Stamp Advisory Committee
c/o Stamp Development U.S. Postal Service Attention: Markes S. Lucius
475 L'Enfant Plaza SW, Rm. 3300
Washington, DC 20260

Salutation
Dear Citizens' Stamp Advisory Committee:

Body
Include the following:
- Introduce yourselves and identify the woman you want to nominate to the committee and tell why.
- Give meaningful examples of her achievements.
- Provide stories or anecdotes about your nominee.
- Tell why the stamp honoring your nominee would generate widespread public and stamp collector interest.
- Sum it up in a closing sentence.

Closing
Yours truly,

Signature
Sign your names

Women's History Month STEM Extensions

Science Extension: Google Doodles

In this extension lesson, students learn about the achievements of Grace Murray Hopper, discuss a Google Doodle that illustrates her accomplishments and create their own doodle. Grace Murray Hopper was one of our nation's first computer programmers. She was known as "Amazing Grace" because of all she achieved in the field of computer science. She is also credited with developing the first computer compiler, which allowed English-like sentences to be input into the computer and be converted into the 1s and 0s that computers understand. She is known as the brains behind COBOL, one of the first modern programming languages. Many of her achievements took place while she was an officer in the United States Navy. When Grace Hopper was 80, she appeared on the David Letterman television show. It is available on YouTube and is also available at the following website: http://blog.usni.org/2015/08/27/video-grace-hopper-on-letterman.

Begin by showing and discussing the following Google Doodle published on December 9, 2013, which would have been Hopper's 107th birthday.
http://www.google.com/doodles/grace-hoppers-107th-birthday
Point out the following facts when viewing the Google Doodle:
1. This Google Doodle was created for what would have been Grace Hopper's 107th birthday and to commemorate Computer Science Education Month established in her honor.
2. Grace is shown programming an early computer, Harvard's Mark II, used during World War II.
3. Grace is using a compiler that she invented to write code in English-like sentences that coverts the code to the 1s and 0s that computers understand. In the Google Doodle, she is using the COBOL language she is credited with developing.
4. The doodle shows a moth exiting the computer. This illustrates the time that Grace was troubleshooting a problem with Harvard's Mark II and found that a moth in the computer caused the problem. Today when programmers fix problems in a computer code, they call it debugging.

Have students work in groups and use the Grace Hopper Google Doodle as a model to create their own Google Doodles illustrating the life of a famous woman scientist as follows:
1. During a brainstorming session, create a class list of women scientists. Below is a list to get you started:
   a. Jane Goodall........................ British primatologist and expert on chimpanzees
   b. Margaret Mead .... Anthropologist
   c. Barbara McClintock .... Nobel Prize winning scientist in physiology who left a legacy of outstanding scientific inquiry.
   d. Rachel Carson .... Marine biologist and environmentalist
   e. Elizabeth Blackwell .... First female American physician in the United States
   f. Mae C. Jemison, M.D. .... Astronaut, doctor, and the first African American to travel in space

43

     g.   Lillian Gilbreth.....................Psychologist and industrial engineer known for her time management and motion studies

     h.   Sally Ride.............................Astronaut and the first American woman in space

     i.   Annie Jump Cannon ....American astronomer classified stars according to temperatures

2. Divide the class into small groups.
3. Have each group research one of the women on the list.
4. Have each group list at least 3 or 4 milestones to include in their Google Doodle.
5. Plan and create a Google Doodle on an 8½" x 11" blank paper for the woman scientist selected, using the group's choice of art tools.
6. Have the groups present their Google Doodles to the class.
7. If possible, scan the doodles so they can be presented in a class computer slide show.

Engineering Extension: Time Management Engineers

This lesson is modeled on the work of Lillian Moller Gilbreth. She was the first woman elected to the National Academy of Engineering. She was born on May 24, 1878 in Oakland, California. She and her husband were important pioneers in the field of industrial engineering and time-motion studies. One of her many accomplishments was to design plans for applying efficiency techniques for homemakers to save them time and energy in their daily life. In addition to becoming famous for her work, she became a celebrity after two of her children wrote the book *Cheaper by the Dozen* that told the story of life with their mother and father. Students become industrial time-management engineers as they work in groups to find how many Women's History month small book lesson cards they can assemble in five minutes. They then conduct a planning session to design new methods for assembling the books to increase speed and efficiency.

Do the following:
1. Discuss Lillian Moller Gilbreth with the class.
2. Tell the class they are going to work in small groups as industrial time-management engineers to plan the most efficient way to get small books ready for Women's History Month mini reports.
3. Divide the class into small groups.
4. Distribute several copies of the Women's History Month Small Book Handout, scissors, markers and crayons to each group.
5. Have the groups follow the directions on the handout to create as many report books as they can in five minutes.
6. When the time is up, have groups count and share their results and the method they used.
7. Have the groups design a plan to create more books in the same amount of time.
8. Give the class a second five-minutes to repeat the directions and create the books more efficiently.
9. Have each group present its plans and an evaluation of its results.
10. Distribute the completed booklets to the class and have each student use one to make a mini report on a woman to honor in celebration of Women's History Month.

Women's History Month Small Book Handout

Instructions:

1. Color the border of the card with at least two colors.
2. Cut the card on the solid black lines
3. Fold the card in half lengthwise along the dotted lines with the page numbers and words on the outside.
4. Make a second fold to complete the booklet.
5. Check to see that the page numbers are displayed correctly.

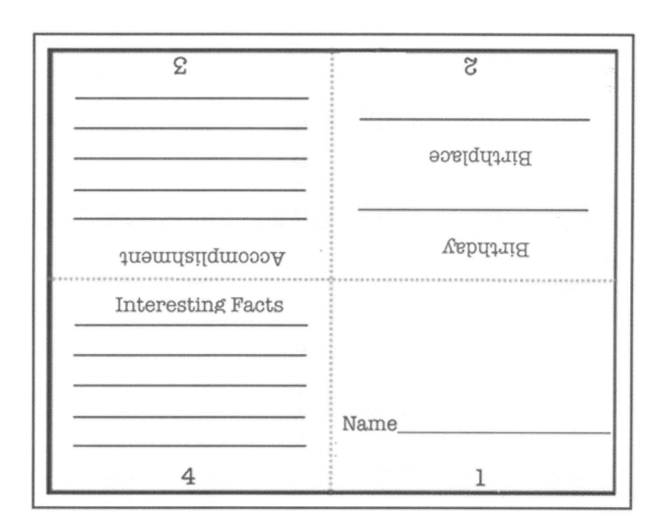

Math Extension: Counting the Milestone Years

In this Women's History Month extension lesson, students solve and create word problems based on milestones achieved by American women in (1) the United States Senate, (2) space and (3) the Supreme Court. Working in pairs, small groups or on their own, students search the Internet to hone their math skills as they learn about meritorious women. When the worksheets are completed, have students share and check their answers. Have students present the word problems they created to the class. Included below is an answer key and suggested websites to find further information.

1. United States Senate
    a. In what year was history made when two California women, Diane Feinstein and Barbara Boxer, were elected to the United States senate at the same time? <u>1992</u>
    b. How many other women were elected with them? <u>two</u>
    c. What fractional number of women elected in that year did the two senators represent? <u>1/2</u>
    http://www.senate.gov/artandhistory/history/minute/year_of_the_woman.htm

2. Space
    a. Who was the first American woman to travel in space? <u>Sally Ride</u>
    b. In what year did she achieve this milestone? <u>1983</u>
    c. When did Eileen Collins become the first women space shuttle pilot? <u>1995</u>
    d. When did she join NASA? <u>1991</u>
    http://www.scientafoundation.com/scientista-spotlights/the-top-6-female-astronauts-every-scientista-should-know-about
    http://starchild.gsfc.nasa.gov/docs/StarChild/whos_who_level2/collins.html
    http://starchild.gsfc.nasa.gov/docs/StarChild/whos_who_level2/ride.html

3. Supreme Court
    a. In what year did George Washington appoint John Jay as the first Supreme Court Justice? <u>1798</u>
    b. Who was the first female Supreme Court justice? <u>Sandra Day O'Connor</u>
    c. When did the first female justice join the Supreme Court? <u>1981</u>
    d. How many years was the Supreme Court all male? <u>183</u>
    https://www.constitutionfacts.com/us-supreme-court/first-chief-justice-john-jay/
    http://www.supremecourt.gov/visiting/SandraDayOConnor.aspx

Counting the Milestone Years

1. **United States Senate**
    a. In what year was history made when two California women, Diane Feinstein and
       Barbara Boxer, were elected to the United States Senate at the same time? _____
    b. How many women were elected with them? _____
    c. What fractional number of women elected in that year did the two senators
       represent? _____
    d. Write a math word problem of your own. _____
       _____

       http://www.senate.gov/artandhistory/history/minute/year_of_the_woman.htm

4. **Space**
    a. Who was the first American woman to travel to space? _____
    b. In what year did she achieve this milestone? _____
    c. When did Eileen Collins become the first women space shuttle pilot? _____
    d. When did she join NASA? _____
    e. Write a math word problem of your own _____
       _____

       http://starchild.gsfc.nasa.gov/docs/StarChild/whos_who_level2/ride.html
       http://starchild.gsfc.nasa.gov/docs/StarChild/whos_who_level2/collins.html

5. **Supreme Court**
    a. In what year did George Washington appoint John Jay as the first Supreme Court
       Justice? _____
    b. Who was the first female Supreme Court justice? _____
    c. When did the first female justice join the Supreme Court? _____
    d. How many years was the Supreme Court all male? _____
    e. Write a math word problem of your own. _____
       _____

       https://www.constitutionfacts.com/us-supreme-court/first-chief-justice-john-jay/
       http://www.supremecourt.gov/visiting/SandraDayOConnor.aspx

Poetry Lesson for Women's Appreciation Month: Praised Be Diana's Fair and Harmless Light

This is the month to praise women for who they are and what they have accomplished. In his poem, Sir Walter Raleigh praises Diana, a powerful Roman goddess of the hunt, the moon, birthing and fertility. He praises her power that moves "the floods." He praises the spirits "her nymphs, with whom she decks the woods." He praises her beauty that will last eternally: "Time wears her not—she doth his chariot guide." In the last two lines of the poem, Raleigh writes that Diana has pure knowledge and people who do not believe in her should dwell with Circes, a minor goddess who is a magician and with her magic spreads lies.

Materials
- Sir Walter Raleigh Biography and his poem *Praised Be Diana's Fair and Harmless Light*
- Word processing software, Google Docs, or desktop publishing software

Plan
- Read and discuss Sir Walter Raleigh's biography and poem.
- Read and discuss the poem using the following questions and discussion points.
  - For what is Diana praised?
  - Why does Diana not grow older?
  - Discuss what the last two lines mean. "A knowledge pure it is her worth to know/With Circes let them dwell that think not so."

Do
Getting Ready to Write
- Conduct a brainstorming session by asking students to list women to praise. Tell students they can praise someone in their own lives such as their mother, or they can praise a mythological woman or a famous person of whom they have knowledge.
  - Who would they praise?
    For example: *mother, aunt, grandmother, mythological woman, historical woman*
  - Continue with the following question and write answers on the board. What would they praise about this woman? Suggest they embellish the praise.
    For example: *Praised be her spirit that lights my life; Praised be her beauty that outshines all the flowers in an English spring garden.*

Writing the Poem
- Students write their own poems following the directions below:
  - Suggest they title their poem "Praise to" and the name of whom they are praising.
  - Begin the first line "Praised be" and add to whom they are praising. Embellish the line with a a praise about the woman.
  - Begin the second line and all consecutive lines with "Praise be her" and add another praise about her.
  - Suggest that students write at least seven praises.

Editing and Publishing
- Have students read and edit poems with partners.
- Students handwrite their poems in fancy penmanship and draw a decorative border.

Sir Walter Raleigh Biography
Circa 1552 – October 29, 1618

Walter Raleigh was born in England. The date of his birth is unknown but historians believe it was 1552. Although his father came from a wealthy family, his family's finances had dwindled by the time Raleigh was born. He attended Oxford University but did not graduate. At the age of 26, he sailed to America with his half-brother, an explorer.

Raleigh served in the army of Queen Elizabeth 1 of England. He fought in Ireland and was honored by the Queen for his service. She rewarded him with knighthood, a large estate in Ireland and the right to establish colonies in America.

Raleigh sailed with a fleet of seven vessels. His 108 men reached Roanoke Island (today part of North Carolina) and established the colony of Virginia. Raleigh was the first person to bring back potatoes and Virginian tobacco to Europe. He was also responsible for making smoking tobacco popular in the European court.

There is a myth that Raleigh once threw his cloak over a mud puddle to protect the queen as she walked by. He repeated this myth in a famous novel. The myth ends with the queen blushing and nodding her head, as she 'hastily passed on, and embarked in her barge without saying a word."

He was loved by Queen Elizabeth for the poems he wrote praising her. When she found out that he was secretly married to one of her maids of honor, she went into a fit of jealous rage. She had Raleigh and his wife imprisoned in the Tower of London.

After his release, he went on two expeditions to the New World searching for El Dorado, a city of gold, which he never found. After the first failure, James 1 put him in prison for plotting against the king. He spent 12 years there, occupying himself by writing books. He was released and after his second failure to find the city of gold, and defying the king's instructions not to attack the Spanish, Raleigh was put back into prison, given the death sentence and executed.

Praised Be Diana's Fair and Harmless Light
by Sir Walter Raleigh

Praised be Diana's fair and harmless light,
Praised be the dews wherewith she moists the ground;
Praised be her beams, the glory of the night;
Praised be her power, by which all powers abound.

Praised be her nymphs, with whom she decks the woods;
Praised be her knights, in whom true honor lives;
Praised be that force by which she moves the floods;
Let that Diana shine, which all these gives.

In heaven queen she is among the spheres;
In aye she mistress-like makes all things pure;
Eternity in her oft change she bears;
She beauty is; by her the fair endure.

Time wears her not—she doth his chariot guide;
Mortality below her orb is placed.
By her the virtue of the stars down slide,
In her is virtue's perfect image cast.

    A knowledge pure it is her worth to know;
    With Circes let them dwell that think not so.

Additional Poem for Women's History Month

In this poem *She Walks in Beauty*, Lord Byron praises the outward and inward beauty of a woman. She is as beautiful as a night with "starry skies." She is also "pure" and spends her days in "goodness" with a mind that is at "peace." In this lesson, students create a water colored painting using the descriptions of the woman in the poem by Byron.

She Walks in Beauty
By Lord Byron

She walks in beauty, like the night
Of cloudless climes and starry skies;
And all that's best of dark and bright
Meet in her aspect and her eyes;
Thus mellowed to that tender light
Which heaven to gaudy day denies.

One shade the more, one ray the less,
Had half impaired the nameless grace
Which waves in every raven tress,
Or softly lightens o'er face;
Where thoughts serenely sweet express,
How pure, how dear their dwelling–place.

And on that cheek, and o'er that brow,
So soft, so calm, yet eloquent,
The smiles that win, the tints that glow,
But tell of days in goodness spent,
A mind at peace with all below,
A heart whose love is innocent.

March – St. Patrick's Day Lessons and Projects

Engineering Lesson: Building a Leprechaun Trap – Cardboard Challenge

This lesson is an adaptation of the Cardboard Challenge activity that began as a response to the film *Caine's Arcade*. The film can be viewed on the cainesarcade.com website. According to legend, every leprechaun has a pot of gold hidden somewhere, and he must give up his treasure to anyone who catches him. In this lesson, students use cardboard boxes, tape, various other supplies and their imaginations as they work together as engineers to plan a leprechaun trap, test out their prototype, make changes to their original idea and build their final trap. They share their finished traps with the class and demonstrate the way it will work to catch a leprechaun.

MATERIALS

- Film, *Caine's Arcade*, parts 1 and 2 from cainesarcade.com
- Cardboard
- Boxes of all shapes and sizes (cereal, shoe)
- Tape (masking, packing, duck)
- Cartons (egg, milk)
- Scissors
- Possible extra materials such as:
  - Toilet paper and paper towel rolls
  - Paints and markers
  - Brushes
  - Bubble wrap
  - Wrapping paper
  - Box cutters
  - Wrapping paper
  - Fabric
  - Pencils
  - Yarn
  - Paper bags
  - Glue

Coeur D'Alene Elementary 3rd Grade

PLAN

- If possible begin the lesson by showing the film *Caine's Arcade* for inspiration. After watching the film, tell students they are going to participate in a cardboard challenge.

- Have students design a cardboard trap to catch a leprechaun.
- Have students create a list of materials they feel will be helpful in the project.
- Students and teacher collect materials and have them in class before the challenge to build a leprechaun trap begins.

Project Description:
- Divide the class into groups.
- Have the groups use the materials available – and their imaginations – to design leprechaun traps.
- Remind students that leprechauns are very sneaky and smart so their traps will have to be clever.
- Tell them they need to make a list of materials they will need and create a design for their traps before they begin building.
- Using the designs they create, have students begin to build the traps.
- Encourage the groups to evaluate their design as they continue to build and make any improvements to the original design as they continue building.
- When the traps are completed, have students demonstrate them for the class.

Coeur D'Alene
3rd Grade Students

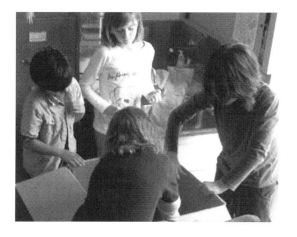

St. Patrick's Day STEM Extensions

Science Extension: Rainbows

Rainbows are fun to learn about. According to Irish folklore, Leprechauns were said to be shoemakers who saved all their profits and hid them in pots at the end of the rainbow. It is thought they put the gold at the end of the rainbow because it's an impossible place to find. Actually, rainbows are full circles of light. When we are on the ground, we can only see the semicircle or arc of the rainbow as it disappears beyond the horizon. Pilots have reported seeing full rainbow circles in flight. Your class can view some of these sightings on the Internet. Try these fun rainbow science activities to help celebrate St. Patrick's Day.

Making A Rainbow

Have your students work in small groups of two or three. If it's a sunny day, each group will need a glass of water, a sheet of white paper and the sun. If the day is not sunny, students can a use flashlight as the sun.

To make a rainbow when the sun is shining, have students do the following:
1. Pour water into the glass filling it close to the top.
2. Place the sheet of white paper on the floor.
3. On a sunny day, hold the glass on the edge of a table so that it is half on and half off, allowing the sun to shine directly through the water to the sheet on the floor.
4. Move the glass and paper around until a rainbow appears on the paper.

To make a rainbow using a flashlight as the sun, have students do the following:
1. Place the white paper on the floor.
2. Pour water into the glass filling it close to the top.
3. Place the glass of water on the paper.
4. Shine the flashlight on the water and move it around until a rainbow appears on the paper.

Following their explorations, discuss the reason rainbows are formed. Explain that light has many colors. When light from the sun or the flashlight passes through the water, the light is broken up into all seven colors of the rainbow.

Richard of York Gave Battle in Vain (ROYGIV)

This mnemonic device helps us remember the colors that make up a rainbow: red, orange, yellow, green, indigo and violet. The letters in the name are the seven colors they see when the sun breaks up the water molecules to create a rainbow. Have the class learn the letters of the rainbow by remembering the mnemonic device or have them create a sentence of their own.

The Right Perspective

Tell the students that in order to see a rainbow, they need to be standing with the sun behind them and the raindrops in front of them. Have students use crayons, markers and or paint to create a picture of themselves standing in the right place to see a beautiful rainbow with its seven colors displayed in an arch.

Technology Extension: St. Patrick's Day Collage

Have your students work in pairs to practice their word processing skills and Internet search skills as they create a St. Patrick's Day collage. The supplies needed are a word processing program such as Microsoft Word, Pages or Google Docs. Show students how to use the picture menu in their word processor, including word wrap, transparency and editing features to move and artistically place the graphics and text.

To make a collage, each pair begins the project by spending a designated amount of time making a list of items to include. Encourage students to include a variety of objects for their collage, including slogans such as Erin Go Baugh; blessings and proverbs such as "A friend's eye is a good mirror;" and graphics such as shamrocks, rainbows and leprechauns.

Next, students search the Internet for images on their list, saving the images to a designated folder on their computer. When all have been selected, have students place them in an artistic arrangement in their word processing program. Encourage students to use all of the picture placing and picture editing features to create an interesting design. Remind them to leave room for text to be added to their arrangement.

Have students print their finished designs using a color printer. Show off the collages by having students mount the pictures and display on a classroom bulletin board.

Math Extension: Charming Math

Lucky Charms cereal debuted in 1963 and for over fifty years has been a favorite at the breakfast table. The cereal features frosted oats along with marshmallow charms (known as "marbits"). In this charming math lesson, students will explore math concepts using boxes of Lucky Charms cereal. Students will experience math skills with graphs, percentages, fractions as well as statistics and probability. This lesson meets standards appropriate for a student's grade level. Children love the marbits in Lucky Charms and it is fun to imagine each of the charms bringing special powers. Although the charms included have changed over the years, it's interesting that only the pink heart remains. Create a chart to share with the class as part of this lesson. Check the box of cereal you are using to see if new marbits have been added. As students estimate, count and sort, they will use these as a reference point.

Charm	Special Power
Hearts	Life
Shooting Starts	Flight
Horseshoes	Speed
Clovers	Luck
Blue Moons	Invisibility
Rainbows	Soar
Balloons	Float
Hourglass	Time

Divide the class into small groups. Give each group member a snack or sandwich size plastic bag. A box of Lucky Charms contains approximately six cups. Snack bags will hold about ½ cup. Groups randomly place the Lucky Charms in the small bags, dividing up the entire box. Have each group member do the following:

1. Create a tally sheet by writing the names of each marshmallow charm in a vertical row on a sheet of paper.
2. Hold up individual bags and have group member estimate how many marshmallows of each kind are mixed into the cereal.
3. Write the total group predictions on a board or chart.
4. After bags have been displayed and predictions are recorded, students individually count and sort the marshmallows in his or her bag and record the results on the tally sheet.
5. Distribute 1" graph paper to each student. Have students transfer individual data from their tally sheet to the graph paper by writing the names of the marshmallow charms on the bottom and coloring each square in the correct column to correspond with the data on the tally sheet.
6. Depending on the math level of the students. Have students do the following computations with the data they created:
   a. Write each result as a fraction of the total charms found.
   b. Reduce the fractions to the lowest common denominator.
   c. Change the fractions to the percentages.
   d. Combine and the group totals and use the results to create statistical information.
   You can continue this lesson by creating stories of the special powers, writing math word problems, and/or researching the history of Lucky Charms cereal.

Poetry Lesson for St. Patrick's Day: Limericks

Both St. Patrick's Day and limericks originated in Ireland. Limericks make a perfect poetry lesson for St. Patrick's Day. This fun and humorous form of poetry began in the 14th century in the Irish town of Limerick. Limericks were made popular by the poet Edward Lear. The limericks in this lesson are named for two Irish towns. Your students will enjoy learning *There Was an Old Man of Kildare* and *There Was an Old Man of Kilkenny* and writing their own limericks.

MATERIALS
- Edward Lear Biography and two of his limericks
- Word processing software, Google Docs, or desktop publishing software

PLAN
- Read and discuss Edward Lear's biography and his limericks.
  - Discuss how limericks are structured.
    - Lines one, two and five rhyme with one another.
    - Lines three and four rhyme with each other.
    - Limericks are humorous.
    - The first line ends with a name or place.
    - The last line repeats the place named in the first line.
  - Read and discuss the selection of limericks to show students how each one of Lear's limericks follows the appropriate limerick rules.

DO
Getting Ready to Write
- During a brainstorming session, ask students the following questions. List their responses on a board or on a chart.
  - What places would they like to use in the first and last lines of their own limerick?
  - Who or what would be at that place?
- Have students participate in writing a group limerick beginning with "There was a" and following the suggested rules.
Writing the Poem
Following the group limerick, students write their own.
Editing and Publishing
- Have students first read to themselves to check their rhyme structure.
- Have students read and edit limericks with partners.
- Plan a limerick reading party where students read their poems and eat green cookies and drink green punch.
- Create a book of class limericks.

Edward Lear Biography
May 12, 1812 – January 29, 1888

Edward Lear was born in Holloway, a small London village. He was second to the youngest of 21 children. Most of his siblings died when they were infants. He lived with his parents until he was four years old. His father, a stockbroker, had financial difficulties. Young Edward moved in with his sister who was 21 years older than he was. He lived with her for the rest of her life.

From the age of five on, he had epileptic seizures. He felt ashamed of his condition and suffered from depression. He had trouble developing relationships.

At 16, he was earning a living by drawing illustrations for the Zoological Society. Later, he was employed by a wealthy man who had a private menagerie. He drew beautiful paintings of his employer's animals.

He loved to travel and created beautiful colored drawings of what he saw in his travels. Queen Victoria even hired him to teach her how to draw.

Lear loved the Italian Mediterranean coast and settled there. He never married but had many close friendships that lasted his entire life. His best friend was his cat, Foss, who died two years before Lear did.

Lear was known as an artist, writer, illustrator, and poet. He was well known for his limericks. They were funny, perhaps hiding his own sadness. His limericks made him famous and he in turn, made limericks famous. Besides his limericks, he also is remembered for the beloved children's classic *The Owl and the Pussycat.*

Limericks
by Edward Lear

There Was an Old Man of Kildare

There was an Old Man of Kildare,
Who climbed into a very old chair;
When he said,-- "Here I stays--
till the end of my days,"
That immovable Man of Kildare.

There Was an Old Man of Kilkenny

There was an Old Man of Kilkenny,
Who never had more than a penny;
He spent all that money,
In onions and honey,
That wayward Old Man of Kilkenny.

Additional Poems for St. Patrick's Day

This humorous poem, *The Leprechaun,* is about being fooled. Leprechauns must give you their "purse of gold" if you capture them. Write a story on how to trick a leprechaun.

The Leprechaun
by Robert Dwyer Joyce

In a shady nook one moonlit night,
A leprechaun I spied
In scarlet coat and cap of green,
A cruiskeen by his side
'Twas tick, tack, tick, his hammer went,
Upon a weeny shoe,
And I laughed to think of a purse of gold,
But the fairy was laughing too.

With tip-toe step and beating heart,
Quite softly I drew night.
There was mischief in his merry face,
A twinkle in his eye;
He hammered and sang with tiny voice,
And sipped the mountain dew;
Oh! I laughed to think he was caught at last,
But the fairy was laughing, too.

As quick as thought I grasped the elf,
"Your fairy purse," I cried,
"My purse?" said he, "'tis in her hand,
That lady by your side."
I turned to look, the elf was off,
And what was I to do?
Oh! I laughed to think what a fool I'd been,
And, the fairy was laughing too.

The lyrics for this famous song, *I'm Looking Over a Four Leaf Clover,* were written in 1924 by Mort Dixon. The music was written by Harry M. Woods. Have you searched for a four-leaf clover? Have you found one? The odds of finding a four leaf clover are 10,000 to one. Children in the Middles Ages believed if they carried a four-leaf clover they would be able to see fairies. Find three more superstitions associated with four leaf clovers.

I'm Looking Over a Four Leaf Clover
by Mort Dixon

I'm looking over a four leaf clover
That I overlooked before
First is the sunshine, the second is rain
Third is the roses that bloom in the lane

There's no need explaining
The one remaining is somebody I adore
I'm looking over a four leaf clover
That I overlooked before

I'm looking over a four leaf clover
That I overlooked before
First is the sunshine, the second is rain
Third is the roses that bloom in the lane

There's no need explaining
The one remaining is somebody I adore
I'm looking over a four leaf clover
That I overlooked before, that I overlooked before

March – Music in Our Schools Month Lessons and Projects

Math Lesson: Fractionated Rhythms

In this lesson students link their understanding of common core math concepts to the beat of musical notes. Students study the fractional values of notes and use these values to review addition and subtraction of fractions. They also learn about equivalent fractions. Students work in groups to create their own songs using four beats per measure. By clapping, stomping, humming and using plastic cups, they perform their compositions for the class.

MATERIALS
- Musical Beats chart
- Projection device
- Pencil, paper
- One plastic cup per student

PLAN
- Project the Musical Beats chart in the front of the room. The notes on the chart are the whole note, half note, quarter note, eighth note, sixteenth note, dotted half note, dotted quarter note, and dotted sixteenth note.
- Depending upon the musical background of students, introduce or review the notes displayed on the chart, one at a time, while pointing to them. Student volunteers are guided to tell whether the note is solid or open; whether it has a vertical line attached or not; whether it has one or more flags attached to the line; and whether it is followed by a dot.
- Have the class join you as you count, clap and say each note as follows:
  - Whole note: four beats (ta-ah-ah-ah)
  - Half note: two beats (ta-ah)
  - Quarter note: one beat (ta)
  - Eighth note: ½ beat (ta-te)
  - Sixteenth note: ¼ beat (tafa-tefe)
  - Dots add half the value of the note to the original note. For example, a dotted half note has three beats. Count, clap and tap the dotted whole, quarter and half notes on the chart.
- Practice counting, humming the beats in the first four measures of the song, "Twinkle, Twinkle Little Star."

DO
- Divide the class into small groups.
- Challenge each group to draw four groups of notes to create four-beat measures showing their equivalent fractional values. Each measure needs to be different than the other three measures. Below is an example of one measure:

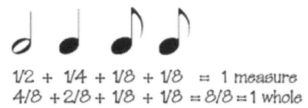

1/2 + 1/4 + 1/8 + 1/8 = 1 measure
4/8 + 2/8 + 1/8 + 1/8 = 8/8 = 1 whole

- Once the four measures are created, the groups use their plastic cup to tap their four-measure creation.

Musical Beats

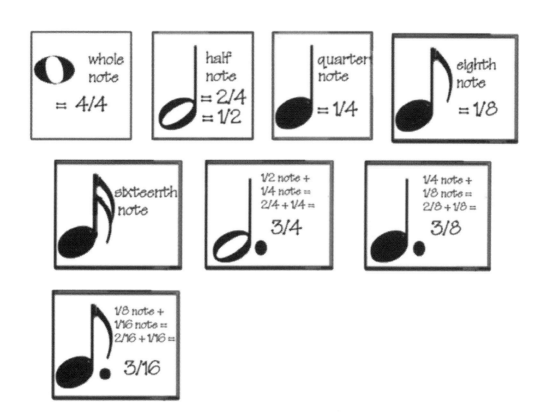

Twinkle Twinkle Little Star

Music in Our Schools Month STEM Extensions

Science Extension: Sound

In this lesson students explore sound, a vibration that begins with a movement such as tapping a pencil, knocking on the door, turning on a faucet or strumming a guitar. The molecules around the movement vibrate and those vibrations cause more vibrations. This is how sound travels. Sound does not travel through outer space because it needs to travel through matter. Since space is a vacuum without matter, space is a soundless place.

Music is present in nature when birds chirp. People also make music by singing and playing instruments. Singers use their diaphragm, larynx and breath in special ways to take advantage of sound vibrations. Over the years, people have created many different instruments that use vibrations to create the special musical sounds we hear when we listen to an orchestra.

This extension pairs well with the engineering extension also in this unit. Once students understand and "see" vibrations at work, they can move on to the engineering extension lesson and create instruments that use these vibrations in a variety of ways. The following experiments are designed to enable students to observe sound vibrations by watching them move through matter present in water, air and land. The experiments can be done together as a whole class with student volunteers, in pairs, or in small groups.

Experiment 1 – Vibrations in the Air

You will need an empty cardboard container with a lid that is shaped in a cylinder (oatmeal and ice cream containers work well), a box cutter or utility knife, a candle in a candle holder and matches.

1. Make a small round hole in the container's lid with the box cutter or knife.
2. Place the container on its side.
3. Light the candle with adult supervision.
4. Hold the container with the hole pointing toward the candle leaving a distance of about 4-6 inches.
5. Lightly tap the bottom of the box.

You should see the candle flicker caused by the movement of the wave of vibrations set off by the tap. These are sound waves. With just the right tap and the right distance, you may able to watch the sound waves cause the candle to go out.

Experiment 2 – Vibrations on Your Eardrum

You will need a large bowl, enough plastic wrap to securely cover and seal the bowl, a handful of uncooked rice, a metal spoon and a baking pan. The vibrations of the rice show what happens to sound when it hits your eardrum.

1. Tightly stretch the plastic wrap over the top of the bowl emulating your eardrum.
2. Place a handful of rice on top of the plastic wrap.
3. Hold the baking pan a few inches from the bowl and bang on it with the spoon.
4. Watch the rice jump. Move the pan a little and hit it again, the rice should jump again.
5. Try hitting the pan with a pencil, ruler and even try singing to the eardrum mock-up.

Experiment 3 - Experiencing How Sound Travels

You will need the following for each pair of students: two paper clips, two plastic cups, approximately six feet of string and an instrument for making holes such as a ballpoint pen or sharp pencil.

1. Make one hole in the bottom of each cup.
2. Tie a paper clip to one end of the string and pull the other end through the inside hole of one cup until the paper clip is tightly secured at the bottom.
3. Pass the loose end of the string through the outside hole of the second cup.
4. Tie the second paper clip to the end of the string on the inside of the cup so it rests securely.
5. Student partners each hold a cup and move away from one anther until the string between the cups is tight.
6. One student holds a cup to his or her ear while the other speaks into his or her cup.
7. The listening student hears what the other is saying through the cup. The speaking student causes his or her paper clip to move. This causes movement in the air particles. The particles hit other particles close to them and they also vibrate causing what are called sound waves.
8. Partners reverse speaking and listening roles and try the experiment again.

Experiment 4 - Kazoo Voice Vibrations

You will be making a cardboard kazoo. You will need a cardboard tube such as a toilet paper or paper towel roll, scissors, wax paper, a pencil and rubber bands.

1. Cut the wax paper into a square that is about an inch larger than the open end of the cardboard tube.
2. Make a pencil hole, about two inches from the end of the tube,
3. Tightly wrap the wax paper around the end securing it with a rubber band.
4. Your finished product is called a kazoo.
5. Hum or speak into your instrument.
6. Open and close the hole with your finger. What does this do to the sound?

The reason the kazoo amplifies your voice is that the sound waves from your voice are actually many different vibrations coming together all at once. These sounds are called harmonics. The combination of the harmonics that make up your voice is what makes it different and easy to identify. The kazoo changes your voice harmonics and thus your voice sounds different.

Technology Extension:
Graphing from Glyphs

In this extension lesson, students complete and use glyphs to collect, organize and graph data about music in their lives. A glyph is a pictorial form of data collection. Students begin by completing a glyph survey. Once the data is collected they tally the results. They work with partners to create graphs to present the results.

Begin by distributing graphs and crayons or markers to the class. Tell students they will be answering survey questions about music in their lives by completing the music glyphs using the Music Glyph Key Handout. Students work in groups to organize and compute the data from the glyphs. Groups report their data to the class while volunteers record the results on the board or on a chart.

Students use a technology tool to present the data in bar, circle or line graphs. Encourage students to use one or more of the online graph creators. Graphs created on two, easy-to-use graph makers, are shown below with their URLs. Students complete their projects by evaluating their graphed results and writing summative statements of their findings.

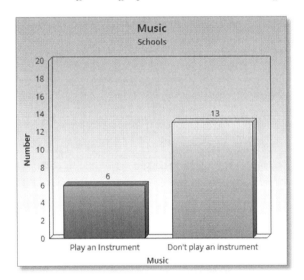

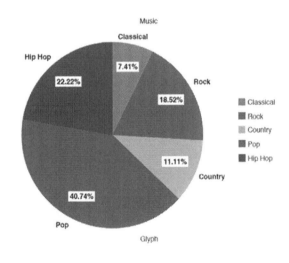

www.chargo.com   https://nces.ed.gov/nceskids/createagraph

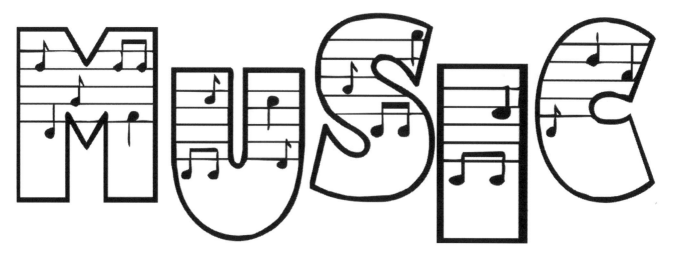

Music Glyph Key Handout

Favorite Kind of Music	
Classical	Color the M red
Rock	Color the M green
Country	Color the M orange
Pop	Color the M purple
Hip Hop/Rap	Color the M blue

Favorite Instrument	
Electric Guitar	Color the U purple
Piano	Color the U pink
Drums	Color the U red
Violin	Color the U green
Saxophone	Color the U yellow

Play a Musical Instrument	
Yes	Color the S orange
No	Color the S blue

Favorite Music Activity	
Singing	Color the I red
Dancing	Color the I green
Listening	Color the I blue
Playing an instrument	Color the I yellow

Performance Attendance	
Opera, symphony, musical, ballet	Color the C orange
Pop concert	Color the C purple
All of the above	Color the C half orange, half purple
None of the above	Color the C green

Engineering Extension: Good Vibrations

In this extension, students become acoustical engineers as they design, analyze and control the sound of the instruments they build. Explain to students that they will be learning how different instruments make music by using air and water vibrations. Divide students into the following four groups: banjo, liquid xylophone, pan flute and soda bottle organ. Distribute the Good Vibrations Handout and the supplies needed to each group. Have group members first follow the specific directions to build their assigned instrument and then modify their instruments by exploring various frequencies and acoustics. Have each group present and play their instruments at the end of the lesson.

Banjo Group

Pint-sized ice cream, cottage cheese or other round container
Heavy cardboard cut to a 1 1/2" x 10" rectangle
Paper fasteners (1/2 inch)
Rubber Bands
Hole punch
Crayons
Scissors

Liquid Xylophone Group

Six glass vessels all the same size and shape. For example,
    jars, bottles, glasses or test tubes in a test tube holder.
Metal and wooden spoons
Measuring cup
Water
Tape
Marker
Food coloring (optional, but recommended)

Pan Flute Group

Straws
Scissors
Ruler
Masking tape
Pen or marker

Soda Bottle Organ

Five or six empty plastic soda pop bottles
Measuring Cup
Water
Food coloring (optional, but recommended)

Good Vibrations Handout

Banjo Group	Liquid Xylophone Group
1. Cut 1 3/4" slits on each side of the carton parallel and near to the top. 2. Slide the 1½" x 10" heavy cardboard through the slots so that it extends 1" from the container on both sides. 3. Punch two holes into each of the extended ends. 4. Put paper fasteners into the holes. 5. Stretch the rubber bands from end to end through the fasteners to create banjo strings. 6. Cut slits in the rim to hold the rubber bands steady. 7. Strum the banjo. 8. Try playing a blue grass song.	1. Place the glass vessels in a row. 2. Tap each empty glass with a metal spoon. Listen to the resulting sound. 3. Measure and pour water into each glass. Fill the first glass with a little water continuing to fill the other glasses by adding a little more to each glass as you move down the row making the final glass practically full. 4. Add optional food coloring to the glasses to better see the water lines. 5. Tap each bottle with the metal spoon, a rubber spatula, a wooden pencil and more. Listen to the sounds they produce. 6. Create a song with your Liquid Xylophone.
Pan Flute Group	**Soda Bottle Organ**
1. Begin with eight straws. 2. Measure and cut the longest straw, making it seven inches long. 3. Measure and cut the remaining seven straws so each is 1/2 inch shorter than the previous. 4. Line them up from biggest to smallest with the tops of the straws all flush in a line. 5. Tape them together. 6. Hold the flat end of the pan flute vertically below your lips. 7. Position your lips as if you are blowing across the tops of a soda pop bottle and blow across the pan flute. 8. With a little practice you can play some of your favorite tunes.	1. Begin with six plastic soda bottles. 2. Practice blowing across the top of an empty bottle to produce a tone. 3. Fill the first bottles with a small amount of water. 4. Fill the next five bottles with water, increasing the water level each time. 5. Arrange the bottles in order from least to most amount of water. 6. Blow on the bottles to determine the tone produced. 7. Adjust the amount of water in each bottle to create a tune.

Poetry Lesson for Music in Our Schools Month: The Violin – A Little Bit Nervous

Vladimir Mayakovsky in a humorous, complex and story-like way presents a character study of the personalities of some of the instruments found in an orchestra. This is the perfect poem to help celebrate Music in the Schools Month. In this lesson, students will think about which instrument in the orchestra reminds them most of themselves and write a poem in which they become that instrument. They will include how they feel about themselves and the other instruments.

Mayakovsky's poem is narrated by the orchestra's conductor. The violin with its "child-like" complaining voice and manner irritates the other members of the orchestra. The members include the instruments and the musicians. At first, the drum tries to soothe the violin: "All right, all right, all right!" But the drum can't take it any longer and slips out going to the "Kuznetsky" a famous street in Moscow. The cymbal with his clashing sound becomes irritated with the violin's noise and says, "What is it, what's all the racket about?" At the end of the poem, the conductor realizes that he loves the violin since it reminds him of himself "we're awfully alike;/I too/always yell." He decides to take the violin home saying, "Let's live together."

MATERIALS
- Vladmir Mayakovsky Biography and his poem *The Violin – A Little Bit Nervous*
- Word processing or desktop publishing software (optional)

PLAN
- Read and discuss Vladimir Mayakovsky's biography and poem.
- Read and discuss the poem using the following possible questions:
    - Why does Mayakovksy choose the violin as the instrument that bursts into sobs?
    - Where is personification used?
    - Who is the narrator?
    - Is the narrator's description of the instruments accurate? If so, why?
    - How does the narrator feel about the violin in the beginning of the poem?
    - How does the voice feel about the violin at the end of the poem and why?

DO
Getting Ready to Write
- Have students brainstorm and discuss the following points. As the class gives their responses list them on the board or on a chart.
    - Have students name the different instruments in an orchestra.
    - Continue the discussion, asking them what type of personalities do each one of these instruments have, depending upon how they sound.
    - Ask students what instrument reminds them most of themselves, and why?
    - What would their instrument say?

Writing the Poem

- Students use the instrument that reminds them most of themselves as the main character in their own poem. Refer to the instrument as "I."
- Title their poem with the name of their selected instrument.
- Continue writing their poem with what they are saying, thinking and doing as their selected instrument.
- In their poems, refer to all other instruments using the pronouns "he" or "she."
- Suggest that they continue with how the other instruments react in speech and action.

Editing and Publishing

- Students read and edit their poems with partners.
- Students write their poems either by hand or in a word processing program.
- Students practice reading their poems mimicking the voice of their instrument.
- Work in groups to record their polished performances.

Vladimir Mayakovsky
July 19, 1893 – April 14, 1930

Vladimir Mayakovsky was born in a small town in Russia. His father was a Cossack, an important member of the Russian army. When Vladimir was 13, his father died and his mother and two sisters moved to Moscow, the capital and largest city in Russia.

Vladimir went to school at the Moscow Gymnasium, a school that spanned grades one through eleven. He dropped out at the age of 15 and joined the underground Social Democratic Labor Party. Because of his involvement with the Party, he was imprisoned three times. He disobeyed prison rules and spent six months in solitary confinement. While in isolation, he began writing poetry.

After Vladimir's release from prison, he attended the Moscow Art School and became an independent thinker and writer. He was politically involved, wanting change in Russia. He believed that through art there could be change. He joined and became a prominent member of the Futurist movement that rejected the art of the past. Believing in this movement, he created a new form of Russian poetry. Vladimir began writing, directing plays and publishing his poetry. He moved to St. Petersburg where he became a leading writer. He appeared in three silent films, one of which he wrote and two he directed.

In the 1920's, Vladimir began traveling through Europe and America. He moved back to Russia for financial reasons. Back in Russia, his public appearances and poetry made him famous and financially successful. He bought a new car and hired a driver. Soviet officials became more irritated about Vladimir's ideas that did not conform with those of the government. He was under constant surveillance. His driver was a secret spy for the Soviets.

Vladimir became more and more critical of the Soviet government. Because of his criticisms, he was not allowed to travel out of Russia. He became very depressed and was found dead with a bullet in his heart. It was said that he committed suicide. Ten days after his death, the criminal investigator on his case was also shot dead.

The Violin - A Little Bit Nervous
by Vladimir Mayakovsky
(translated from the Russian text by Dorian Rottenberg)

The violin got all worked up, imploring
then suddenly burst into sobs,
so child-like
that the drum couldn't stand it:
All right, all right, all right!"
But then he got tired, couldn't wait till the violin ended,
slipped out on the burning Kuznetsky
and took flight.
The orchestra looked on, chilly,
while the violin wept itself out
without reason
or rhyme,
and only somewhere,
a cymbal, silly,
kept clashing:
"What is it,
what's all the racket about?"
and when the helicon,
brass-faced, sweaty,
hollared:
"Crazy!
Crybaby!
Be still!"
I staggered,
on to my feet getting,
and lumbered
over the horror-stuck music stands,
yelling,
"Good God"
why, I myself couldn't tell;
then dashed, my arms round the wooden neck to fling:
"You know what, violin,
we're awfully alike;
I too
always yell,
but can't prove a thing!"
The musicians commented,
contemptuously smiling:
"Look at him-
come to his wooden-bride –
tee-hee!"
But I don't care –
I'm a good guy-
"You know, what, violin,
let's live together,
eh?"

Additional Poems for Music in Our Schools Month

This poem, *Master of Music,* glorifies art and eulogizes a conductor who died. Henry Van Dyke writes that although the hand that waved the wand is no longer here, the rich orchestral sounds remain alive in the hearts of people who have heard the music. In this lesson, students listen to an orchestral recording. Brahms' symphonies and Beethoven's symphonies are ones that have the effect on the human spirit that Van Dyke describes in his poem. After they've listened to a recording, they write about why the sounds they hear will never be forgotten.

Master of Music
by Henry Van Dyke

Glory of architect, glory of painter, and sculptor, and bard,
Living forever in temple and picture and statue and song,
Look how the world with the lights that they lit is illumined and starred,
Brief was the flame of their life, but the lamps of their art burn long!

Where is the Master of Music, and how has he vanished away?
Where is the work that he wrought with his wonderful art in the air?
Gone, -- it is gone like the glow on the cloud at the close of the day!
The Master has finished his work, and the glory of music is -- where?

Once, at the wave of his wand, all the billows of musical sound
Followed his will, as the sea was ruled by the prophet of old:
Now that his hand is relaxed, and his rod has dropped to the ground,
Silent and dark are the shores where the marvelous harmonies rolled!

Nay, but not silent the hearts that were filled by that life-giving sea;
Deeper and purer forever the tides of their being will roll,
Grateful and joyful, O Master, because they have listened to thee,
The glory of music endures in the depths of the human soul.

This poem, *Music* by Charles Baudelaire, is about the power of music. What power does music evoke? Ask students to write about their favorite song. How does the song speak to them?

Music
by Charles Baudelaire
Music doth uplift me like a sea
Towards my planet pale,
Then through dark fogs or heaven's infinity
I lift my wandering sail.

With breast advanced, drinking the winds that flee,
And through the cordage wail,
I mount the hurrying waves night hides from me
Beneath her sombre veil.

I feel the tremblings of all passions known
To ships before the breeze;
Cradled by gentle winds, or tempest-blown

I pass the abysmal seas
That are, when calm, the mirror level and fair
Of my despair!

Stephen Vincent Benet in his poem *Music* describes the scenes he hears while his friend plays the piano. Students read the poem and name the instruments they recognize in the poem.

Music
by Stephen Vincent Benet

My friend went to the piano; spun the stool
A little higher; left his pipe to cool;
Picked up a fat green volume from the chest;
And propped it open.
Whitely without rest,
His fingers swept the keys that flashed like swords,
. . . And to the brute drums of barbarian hordes,
Roaring and thunderous and weapon-bare,
An army stormed the bastions of the air!
Dreadful with banners, fire to slay and parch,
Marching together as the lightnings march,
And swift as storm-clouds. Brazen helms and cars
Clanged to a fierce resurgence of old wars
Above the screaming horns. In state they passed,
Trampling and splendid on and sought the vast –
Rending the darkness like a leaping knife,
The flame, the noble pageant of our life!
The burning seal that stamps man's high indenture
To vain attempt and most forlorn adventure;
Romance, and purple seas, and toppling towns,
And the wind's valiance crying o'er the downs;
That nerves the silly hand, the feeble brain,
From the loose net of words to deeds again
And to all courage! Perilous and sharp
The last chord shook me as wind shakes a harp!
. . . And my friend swung round on his stool, and from gods we were men,
"How pretty!" we said; and went on with our talk again.

MARCH LEARNING STANDARDS
Common Core Math

3.MD.B.3 – Draw a scaled picture graph and a scaled bar graph to represent a data set with several categories. Solve one and two –steps.	Graphing from Glyphs
4.NF.B.3.D – Solve word problems involving addition and subtraction of fractions referring to the same whole and having like denominators.	Fractionated Rhythms
5.NF.A.1 – Add and subtract fractions with unlike denominators by replacing given fractions with equivalent fractions in such a way as to product an equivalent sum or difference of fractions with like denominators.	Fractionated Rhythms
6.SP.B.5 – Summarize numerical data sets in relation to their context.	Charming Math
6.RP.A.3.C – Find a percent of a quantity as a rate per 100 (e.g., 30% of a quantity means 30/100 times the quantity); solve problems involving finding the whole, given a part and the percent.	Graphing from Glyphs

Common Core Language Arts – Literature

RL.3.6 – Distinguish their own point of view from that of the narrator or those of the characters.	*The Caterpillar* by Robert Graves
RL.4.4 – Determine the meaning of words and phrases as they are used in a text including those that allude to significant characters found in mythology.	*Praised Be Diana's Fair and Harmless Light* by Sir Walter Raleigh
RL.5.3 – Compare and contrast two or more characters, settings or events in a story or drama, drawing on specific details in the text.	*The Violin A Little Bit Nervous* by Vladimir Mayakovzsky
RL.6.7 – Compare and contrast the experience of reading a story, drama or poem to listening to or viewing an audio or live version of the text including contrasting what they "see" and "hear" when reading the text to what they perceive when they listen or watch.	*Spring Carol* by Robert Louis Stevenson

Common Core Language Arts – Writing

W.3.5 – With guidance and support from peers and adults develop and strengthen writing as needed by planning, revising and editing.	*Praised Be Diana's Fair and Harmless Light* by Sir Walter Raleigh
W.4.2.D – Use precise language and domain specific vocabulary to inform about or explain the topics.	*Music* by Stephen Vincent Benet.
W.5.3.D – Use concrete words and phrases and sensory details to convey experiences and events precisely.	*Spring Carol* by Robert Louis Stevenson
W.6.2.E – Establish and maintain a formal style.	*Limericks* by Edward Lear

MARCH LEARNING STANDARDS
ISTE Technology Standards 2015

ISTE.1 – Creativity and innovation - Students demonstrate creative thinking, construct knowledge and develop innovative products and processes using technology.	Lesson – Wall of Fame – In honor of Women's History Month students work in pairs to select and nominate a famous woman to be commemorated on a United States postage stamp. They use drawing, painting and word processing software to design a stamp and place it on a classroom *Women's Wall of Fame*.
ISTE.2 – Communication and collaboration – Students use digital media and environments to communicate and work collaboratively, including at a distance, to support individual learning and contribute to the learning of others.	Lesson – Vivaldi's *Spring Awakening* – Students work in cooperative learning groups to design a music and video presentation of *Vivaldi's Spring Awakening*.
ISTE.3 – Research and information fluency – Students apply digital tools to gather, evaluate and use information.	Lesson – St. Patrick's Day Collage Lesson – Counting the Milestone Years
ISTE.4 – Critical thinking, problem solving and decision making – Students use critical thinking skills to plan and conduct research, manage projects, solve problems, and make informed decisions using appropriate digital tools and resources.	Lesson – Graphing from Glyphs –Students begin by completing a glyph survey. Once the data is collected they tally the results. They work with partners to create graphs to present the results.

NGSS and ETS1 Science and Engineering Standards 2015

3-5-ETS1-1. – Define a simple design problem reflecting a need or a want that includes specified criteria for success and constraints on materials, time, or cost.	Time Management Engineers – Students become industrial time-management engineers as they work in groups to find how many Women's History month small book lesson cards they can assemble in five minutes in assembly line fashion.
3-5-ETS1-2. – Generate and compare multiple possible solutions to a problem based on how well each is likely to meet the criteria and constraints of the problem.	Building a Leprechaun Trap – Cardboard Challenge – Students use cardboard boxes, tape, various other supplies and their imaginations as they work together as engineers to plan a leprechaun trap.
3-5-ETS1-3. – Plan and carry out fair tests in which variables are controlled and failure points are considered to identify aspects of a model or prototype that can be improved.	Good Vibrations – In this extension, students become acoustical engineers as they design, analyze and control the sound of the instruments they build.
4-LS1-1 – Construct an argument that plants and animals have internal and external structures that function to support survival, growth, behavior, and reproduction.	Invent an Insect – Students use their knowledge of the characteristics that identify insects and the various habitats in which insects live to create a habitat diorama and invent an insect to live in the diorama
NGSS MS / ETS1-2 – Evaluate completing design solutions using a systematic process to determine how well they meet the material and constraints of the problem.	Building a Leprechaun Trap – Students will work in groups to determine design elements necessary to construct the plans for a backyard garden.

April Monthly Holidays

Alcohol Awareness Month • Cancer Control Month • Child Abuse Prevention Month • International Guitar Month • Keep America Beautiful Month • Listening Awareness Month • Mathematics Education Month • Month of the Young Child • Multicultural Communication Month • National Anxiety Month National Cable Month • National Food Month • National Garden Month • National Home Improvement Month • National Humor Month • National Knuckles Down Month • National Occupational Therapy Month • National Welding Month • National Woodworking Month • Pets Are Wonderful Month • Prevention of Cruelty to Animals Month • Stress Awareness Month • Thai Heritage Month • Un-huh Month

April Weekly Holidays

First Week of April
Cherry Blossom Festival • Bat Appreciation Week • Medic Alert Week • National Birthparents Week • National Reading a Road Map Week • Publicity Stunt Week • Straw Hat Week • Week of the Young Child •

Second Week of April
Be Kind to Animals Week • Harmony Week • National Building Safety Week • National Garden Week • National Guitar Week • National Home Safety Week • National Library Week • National Medical Week • TV Turnoff Week

Third Week of April
Bike Safety Week • Boys' and Girls' Club Week • Lefty Awareness Week • Library Forgiveness Week • National Bubble Gum Week • National Coin Week • National Police Week • National Volunteer Week • National Week of the Ocean • Pan American Week

Last Week of April

Big Brother and Big Sister Appreciation Week • Canada-U.S. Goodwill Week • Consumer Protection Week • Egg Salad Week • Forest Week • Intergenerational Week • Jewish Heritage Week Keep American Beautiful Week • National Give-a-Sample Week National TV-Free Week • National YMCA Week • Professional Secretaries Week • Reading is Fun Week • Teacher Appreciation Week (begins the last Monday) • Week of the Young Child

April Moveable Holidays

Tater Day (It's Sweet Potatoes)....................................first Monday

National Day of Hope... first Wednesday

National Walking Day .... first Wednesday

Every Day is Tag Day ....first Saturday

International Fun at Work Day..................first Thursday in April

National Be Kind to Lawyers Day ....second Tuesday

Audubon Day...second Friday

Slow Art Day .... second Saturday

Astronomy Week ....the week of the first quarter moon

Professional Secretaries Day ....Wednesday of the last full week

Take Our Daughters and Sons to Work Day........ fourth Thursday

National Hairball Awareness Day .... last Friday

Arbor Day .... last Friday

Bird Day .... last Friday

Eeyore's Birthday Day ....last Saturday

Save the Frogs Day..last Saturday

Sense of Smell Day ....last Saturday

Penguin Day ....last Saturday

April Days for STEM Makers and Poets

Day		Make and Do
1	April Fool's Day	April Fool's Day dates back hundreds of years. Some interesting and fun pranks and hoaxes happened in recent times. For example, in 1957, Swiss farmers reported to be harvesting a record spaghetti crop. The newscast on the BBC showed footage of people pulling noodles from trees. In 1996, Taco Bell announced that it had purchased the Liberty Bell and were renaming it the Taco Liberty Bell. Visit the online Museum of Hoaxes at hoaxes.org and select the April Fool's Day menu. Read some of the top 100 hoaxes of all time. Which ones are your favorites? Write up a hoax for the museum.
2	National Peanut Butter and Jelly Day	The average American consumes over 1,500 peanut butter and jelly sandwiches before they graduate from high school. In the early 1900s, peanut butter was a delicacy served in the finest of dining establishments. Originally paired with cheese, watercress, or celery, peanut butter met jelly in a 1901 recipe published in the Boston Cooking School Magazine of Culinary Science and Domestic Economics. Today, think outside of the jar and adapt a recipe for peanut butter and jelly cupcakes, French toast, pie, fudge, sushi or whatever else you can dream up. Print your recipe along with an illustration for a class peanut butter and jelly book.
3	Find a Rainbow Day	Make a rainbow using a glass of water, a sunny day or flashlight, and a piece of white paper. Fill the glass with water and place on the paper. Move the flashlight around until you see a rainbow. Why does this happen? Light is made of many colors and the rainbow is an optical phenomenon caused by reflection, dispersion and refraction in water droplets. The sequence most remembered is Sir Isaac Newton's red, orange, yellow, green, blue, indigo and violet. This becomes the mnemonic, "Richard Of York Gave Battle In Vain" (ROYGBIV). After you make your rainbow, created a new mnemonic for ROYGBIV.

4	Vitamin C Day	Vitamin C, also known as ascorbic acid, is a nutrient found in some foods. Celebrate Vitamin C by learning about the foods that have it and the amount needed for good health. The amount you need changes with age and gender. Research the amount of Vitamin C you need per day for your age group. Vitamin C is found in fruits (especially citrus) and many vegetables. Make a chart displaying the amount needed, an illustration of foods that provide you with Vitamin C and the amount found per serving for your good health.
5	Read a Roadmap Day	Roadmaps may have been drawn as early as 1160 BC in Ancient Egypt. Maps were sold as consumer goods as early as the sixteenth century. In the 1920s, oil companies distributed road maps as promotional tools. Today, web mapping tools are a new form of cartography. Web maps deliver up-to-date information in real time, can be personalized and don't need to be printed and distributed. Create an Internet roadmap from your school to the nearest Science museum. What will you see along the way? Write your directions in a guidebook, illustrated with street directions and pictures from the Internet. Create your guidebook in word processing software and save as a pdf (portable document format) for easy electronic distribution.
6	Post-it Notes Day	Dr. Spencer Silver, a scientist at 3M tried to develop a strong adhesive in 1968. He promoted his "solution without a problem" until colleague Art Fry came up with the idea of using Silver's adhesive to anchor a bookmark. The use of yellow paper was an accident, selected because a fellow team of researchers had a lot of yellow scrap paper. Marketed as "Press 'n Peel" with disappointing results, they soon became "Post-it Notes" in 1980. Discover the many inventive ways to use Post-its by Google searching in both Google and Google Images. Create a list of ten inventive Post-it Projects and create a slideshow of Post-it images.

7	Metric System Day	The Metric System of decimal measurement was developed in the 18th century in France and became part of French law on this day in 1795. The "metrification" of America has been tried unsuccessfully since the 1800s. The United States, Burma and Liberia are countries that today do not use the metric system. In our global society, American business encounters numerous problems as we try to do business with the rest of the world. The metric system uses multiples and sub-multiples of decimals (tens). Working in a group, define millimeter, centimeter, meter, and kilometer. Compare the following to their metric counterparts, an inch, a yard, and a mile. Create a worksheet that will show what you've learned. For example, which is longer, a mile or a kilometer?
8	Zoo Lovers Day	Children of all ages love zoos. Historically, known as Zoological Gardens or menageries, modern day zoos date back to the 1750s in Vienna. What is your favorite animal at the zoo? Although most animals you will find in a zoo are not endangered, there are many endangered animals that are at an immediate risk of becoming extinct. There are several ways that scientists are focusing their efforts: habitat restoration, assisted reproduction, and captive breeding efforts, among others. What do the following scientists do and how can they assist endangered species – biologists, ecologists, veterinarians and geneticists?
9	Name Yourself Day	Onomastics is the scholarly study of naming. Today become an onomastic expert and name yourself. You will find all kinds of lists of names on the Internet. For example, the most popular boy and girl names, gemstone names, British royal names, Baby Boomer names and more. The Social Security Administration website (https://www.ssa.ogv/oact/babynames) lets you look up the most popular names for every birth year after 1879. Find five different points in time and compare the top twenty names by placing them in a spreadsheet. How have they changed? What name would you select for yourself? Why? What does your selected name mean? What does your real name mean?

10	Safety Pin Day	The safety pin was patented in 1849 by mechanic Walter Hunt. He sold his patent to the W.R. Grace and Company for $400 (that's about $11,000 in today's dollars). In the years that followed, they made millions of dollars on his invention. Make a simple toy motor. Attach a pin to both the negative and positive sides of a battery. Place a magnet on top of the battery and suspend a small amount of coiled copper wire between the two ends of the safety pin. What makes the coil spin continuously? Take a look on YouTube at https://www.youtube.com/watch?v=oRSU4FnUSrA
11	National Pet Day	Everyone loves man's best friend and a host of other household pets. Approximately 37 to 47 percent of U.S. households have a dog and 30 to 37 percent have a cat. Learn about the problem of overpopulation of pets. Animal shelters in your community take care of dogs, cats, birds and other small animals such as hamsters, rabbits and guinea pigs. Animal shelters are overflowing with over seven million animals each year. Create a poster to encourage people to adopt their next pet from a shelter. If possible, invite an animal control officer to your classroom to learn more about solving pet overpopulation.
12	International Day of Human Space Flight	Russian Yuri Gagarin was the first man in space on this day in 1961. In 2011, the United Nations declared this day the "International Day of Human Space Flight." In the future, you might want to become a space engineer. Look at some pictures of the current modules on the International Space Station. If you were planning the design of module for you to live in, what would it look like? Draw your module. As you prepare to go, you are allowed to take your backpack. What would you pack?

13	Scrabble Day	One hundred million sets of Scrabble have been sold worldwide dating back to 1948. Over a million new sets are sold each year. If you're lucky enough to have the right letters, spelling the word oxyphenbutazone in a single play of Scrabble will give you the highest possible scoring word on a Scrabble board. Read about the history of Scrabble at http://www.scrabble-assoc.com/info/history.html. Have a Scrabble tournament today.
14	Look Up in the Sky Day	It's a bird, It's a plane, no, it's look up in the sky day! Stare up at the morning sky for five minutes and appreciate everything you see. Takes some pictures, list what you see and write your impressions. Using one of the star gazing apps and a smart phone, iPad or iPod device, find the position of the stars and the constellations where you live. There are many free apps to choose from including: Star Chart, SkyView Free, or Star Tracker.
15	National Library Day	Set up a behind the scenes tour of your local library. Interview your school and community librarian with a set of prepared questions. For example, how is your library preparing for the future? What influenced you to become a librarian? What are the most popular books in your library?
16	Day of the Mushroom	Mushroom-cultivation is the new rage according to the Wall Street Journal. With a mushroom cultivation kit, you can bring the growing of edible mushrooms indoors. This hobby is mushrooming each year. You can buy a kit from Fungi Perfecti at www.fungi.com or other online stores. Starting with a block of sawdust and a pan, you will be off and running. Soon you will have several meals worth of shiitakes, pearl oyster mushrooms or meaty maitakes, among others. There are many to choose from. Mushrooms are not a plant; they are a type of fungus. Draw the basic anatomy of a mushroom and answer these questions. How are mushrooms different from other plants? How do they absorb food from their environment? How do they germinate?

17	National Haiku Poetry Day	A short form of Japanese poetry is known as the haiku. It has three lines arranged as 5, 7 and 5 syllables for a total of 17. Haikus are written about a season of the year and do not use similes or metaphors. They don't necessarily name the season, but imply the season through word choice. Working in triads, write a spring haiku together. Each member of the triad writes a spring haiku of his or her own.
18	Animal Crackers Birthday Day	An animal cracker is a small cookie baked in the shape of a zoo or circus animal. A box of animal crackers is usually filled with lions, tigers, bears and elephants. They are slightly sweet and light in color, but there are also frosted and chocolate flavor varieties as well. They started in England in the nineteenth century and made their way to America in 1902. There have been 37 different animals included over the years in Barnum's Animal Crackers with the koala added on the 100th birthday in 2002. Take apart a box of animal crackers. In a group, list, count and graph the animals contained. Decide as a group which animal should be the next to get its own cracker.
19	National Garlic Day	Today we celebrate nature's stinking rose that is often also known as nature's wonder drug. Garlic was native to central Asia and dates back over 6,000 years. There is an old Welsh saying that may have merit: "Eat leeks in March and garlic in May, then the rest of the year, your doctor can play." There is folklore surrounding garlic that is both fact and superstition. Find five garlic facts and five garlic superstitions.
20	Volunteer Recognition Day	School volunteers are worth their weight in gold. It's important to appreciate your volunteers as they give their time and effort helping students and faculty on a daily basis. Brainstorm a list of words that express gratitude and appreciation. Who volunteers at your school? What do they do? Write thank-you notes to school volunteers and present them on this special day.

21	Kindergarten Day	Kindergarten Day celebrates the birthday of Friedrich Froebe born on this day. and He started the first kindergarten in 1837 in Germany. Froebe created geometric building blocks and pattern activity blocks to use with young learners. Have your class develop a list of activities to share with a kindergarten class. For example you may wish to present an art lesson, put on a play, read stories or play a game on the yard.
	National Jelly Bean Day	For National Jelly Bean Day, complete a Jelly Bean Investigation designed to delight your taste buds as you explore two types of sensory processes: tasting and smelling. Before you begin your Jelly Bean Investigation, disinfect your work area and wash your hands. Do not touch any of the jelly beans that will be eaten by someone else. Use a plastic spoon to pick up and place in a person's hand. Begin by understanding that scientists refer to taste as the sensation produced as food meets our tongue's taste buds. Our taste buds can identify five basic taste sensations: sweet, sour, bitter, salty and savory (sometimes called unami and responding to monosodium glutamate). Smell is the sensation from food odors contacting the lining of our nose. We are able to distinguish among thousands of odors. How important will smell be in identifying the flavor of a jelly bean? Close your eyes and have a partner give you a jelly bean as you hold your nose tightly. Chew for 15 seconds and identify the flavor. What happens when you let go of your nose after 15 seconds? How many flavors can you identify?

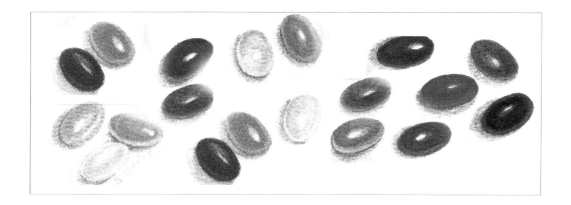

23	Movie Theater Day	The first movie theater was founded in Los Angeles in 1902 and grand opulent movie palaces were built in the 1910s and 20s across America. In 1927, Grauman's Chinese opened in Hollywood and over the years, movie star footprints have been placed in cement. Candy and eventually popcorn became part of the movie going experience during the depression. Theaters have changed over the years, becoming multiplexes, adding 3D, surround sound, Cinerama, Smell-O-Vision and other ploys to bring audiences to the movies. What will the movie theater of the future look-like? Sketch a schematic drawing of your future theater and label the various conveniences and additions your theater will include.
24	National Teach Your Children to Save Day	In your lifetime, you will make four important money choices: to save, to spend, to donate and to invest. Today we learn about saving and compounding interest. When you save money in a bank account with compounding interest, your savings earn money on both your saved amount (known as the principal) and on the interest. That is why saving consistently and starting early will lead to greater returns. This lesson starter is great for students in grade five and above. What will you have at the end of five years? For younger students, find a compounding interest calculator on the web and see if you can answer the same question. Using a spreadsheet, build your own compounding interest calculator as you show what happens by saving $10 a week for 52 weeks. Show what happens if you earn 5% interest, assuming that the interest is paid once a year. What do you have in five years? Assume that your interest is paid every four weeks, what will you have at the end of one year? What will you have at the end of five years? Assume that the interest compounds daily, what will you have at the end of the year?

25	Telephone Day	The modern telephone came about because of the work of many people. However, on this day in 1876, Alexander Graham Bell introduced the telephone. Today we carry our telephones in our pockets. Make a timeline of the changing world of the telephone. Research and identify at least five events to place on your timeline with pictures and images. Use images from the web and provide the year and a few sentences about each of your selections. You can make your timeline by hand, or by using a word processing computer program. Spreadsheet programs also work well for timelines. There are several timeline generators available free on the web that you may also wish to explore.
26	Audubon Day	Today we celebrate the work of John James Audubon who was born on this day in 1785. Audubon was an ornithologist, painter and naturalist who completed a book with over 700 bird species. What makes a bird different from other animals? Birding is a popular pastime. Take a bird walk today. Note the birds you see and sketch pictures of those that you spot.
27	Morse Code Day	Samuel Morse, born on this day in 1791, was the inventor of the Morse Code. The Morse Code is an alphabet where letters are made up of short signals of either light or sound. Telegraphs transmit messages in Morse Code. In 1844 it revolutionized long-distance communication. You can learn Morse Code by visiting this site and printing the Morse Code listening tool: http://www.learnmorsecode.com. By practicing a minute every day, you will soon be an expert. Note that letters more frequently used have simpler dots and dashes. Infrequently used letters like "Q" have longer, more complex code. Try writing your name in Morse Code's dots and dashes. Can you write a complete sentence? Do internet research to determine why SOS is used as an international distress call.

```
1 ● ─ ─ ─ ─        6 ─ ● ● ● ●
2 ● ● ─ ─ ─        7 ─ ─ ● ● ●
3 ● ● ● ─ ─        8 ─ ─ ─ ● ●
4 ● ● ● ● ─        9 ─ ─ ─ ─ ●
5 ● ● ● ● ●        0 ─ ─ ─ ─ ─
```

28	Great Poetry Reading Day	Today we celebrate poetry. Poetry is believed to be some of the oldest written works. Plan a Poetry Reading Day. Each student selects a poem and reads it to the class. Practice in small groups to clearly present the poem. You may wish to use props. For older children, today is a great day to memorize and present your poem.
29	Zipper Day	The zipper was mass produced for the first time during World War I. Billions of zippers are manufactured each year. Zippers were not always successful and it took a lot of engineering and tinkering to get it right. The zipper has an interesting history, read it at: http://www.thomasnet.com/articles/hardware/zipper-history Did you know zippers were named because of the sound they made as they open and close? How many uses of zippers can you find in your classroom? In your bedroom? In your kitchen? For inventive thinkers, can you think of a new or unusual way to use a zipper?
30	Bugs Bunny Day	What's up doc? Bugs Bunny first appeared in a short cartoon, released on April 30, 1938. The legendary Mel Blanc was the voice of Bugs Bunny for almost 50 years. Bugs appeared in *Looney Tunes* and *Merrie Melodies* and was the second cartoon character to have a star on the walk of fame in Hollywood (Mickey Mouse was the first). Bugs is a carrot-chewing, clever rabbit who outsmarts anyone who tries to annoy him, including Elmer Fudd, Wile E. Coyote, and the Tasmanian Devil, among others. Watch some YouTube videos of Bugs Bunny. Download a picture of Bugs from the web. There are many printable Bugs Bunnies that you can download, print and color. Cut him out and make a stop-animation movie of Bugs. Create your background in a drawing program or in Kid Pix. Use a digital device on a stand or a tripod to record the images of Bugs Bunny as he moves across your backdrop.

Children and Nature Awareness Month
Science Lesson: Nature Journaling
Poetry Lesson: The Gladness of Nature
by William Cullen Bryant
Students observe, take records and reflect by keeping nature journals as they pay attention to details and make scientific observations. In the poetry lesson they delight in the poet's nature observations.

Earth Day Lessons and Projects
Technology Lesson:
Earth Day Public Service Announcements (PSAs)
Poetry Lesson: The Cloud
by Percy Bysshe Shelley
Making Earth a healthier place for all living things is the subject of Earth Day Public Service Announcements. Shelley's poem explores the water cycle and the delicate balance of nature.

Poetry Month Lessons and Projects
Engineering Lesson: Drinking Straw Bands
Poetry Lesson: Introduction to Songs of Innocence
by William Blake
Student engineers design reed instruments from drinking straws and make music. The drinking straw bands perform their songs along with poems they write after studying Blake's magical world of a piper.

Math Awareness Month
Math Lesson: Math in the Real World Scavenger Hunt
Poetry Lesson: Arithmetic
by Carl Sandburg
Student groups participate in a math scavenger hunt and learn how math exists in their daily lives. Sandburg's Arithmetic uses humor to present the joys and frustrations with math and numbers.

April – Children and Nature Awareness Month Lesson and Projects
Science Lesson: Nature Journaling

In this lesson, students take a scientific look at nature and hone their skills in observation, record taking and reflection, while experiencing the natural world. In addition to keeping nature journals in the classroom and around the school, they will be encouraged to take nature journeys with their friends and family and continue to record their experiences. As they journey, they will become adept at paying attention to details and making scientific observations. They will learn to look closely at nature, perhaps concentrating on a caterpillar crawling on a leaf or a snail eating a leaf.

MATERIALS
- Journals
- Pencils with erasers
- Natural objects such as rocks, leaves, insects and so on
- Timer
- Colored pencils, crayons, and other drawing tools

PLAN
- Ask students to bring items from nature they find around their home to class.
- Pass out journals and pencils to each student.
- Students write their name on the inside front cover of the journal.
- Students place the nature objects next to them on their desks. Set a timer for one minute. During that time, students sketch one of their nature items. This gives students practice in drawing quickly.
- Remind students that sketching and observing nature are skills that improve with practice.
- Students turn their object in a different direction. Set the timer once again as students quickly sketch the object one more time.
- Next have students write descriptions of the object next to their sketch. Help them hone their observation skills by having them write about the size, color, weight, and special features of their object.

DO
- Students bring their journals and pencils outside to explore the natural environment around the school.
  - Select an interesting space around the school.
  - Sit the class in a circle or square.
  - Every other student turns so they are facing in opposite directions.
  - Students write the date and description of where they are sitting on a new journal page. For example: April 1st, in the school garden, facing north. Repeat for each new journal entry.

- During a five-minute silent time, have students concentrate on the nature surrounding them as they sketch and write their observations on a journal page. Encourage them to pay attention to all their senses as they record their observations.
- At the end of five minutes, give students time to share and discuss their observations.
- Students turn so they are facing the opposite direction and repeat the above activity.
- Save classroom time for students to refine their pages. They may color their sketches, expand their descriptions and/or find additional facts.
- Students bring their journals home for a week to explore the natural environment around their neighborhood.
  - Encourage them to involve friends and family members by asking them to go on a nature walk.
  - Each time they go, have them write an entry in their journal.
  - Remind them to begin each entry with the date and description of their location.
  - Decorate and add facts to their entry when they come back inside.
- After a week has passed, have students bring their journals back to school.
  - Working in small groups, students share their entries.
  - The journals may be placed in your class library.

Children and Nature Awareness Month
STEM Extensions

Technology Extension:
Going on a Camera Walk – Street Photography

One objective of Children and Nature Awareness Month is to encourage children and their families to experience the benefits of being outdoors. In this extension students will work in small groups to take digital photographs of interesting natural objects and outdoor activities they observe during the course of the day. They will import the photos into presentation software programs such as PowerPoint, Google Docs, or Keynote to create artistic slideshows. This is a two-day project.

On Day One

1. Gather as many digital camera devices as possible by collecting those available at the school site. Ask students to bring in cameras and other picture taking devices from home.
2. Divide the class into small photo groups and distribute digital devises to each group.
3. During a class discussion, make a list of some photographic opportunities to take advantage of during the school day. Examples: A beautiful view, friends telling secrets, a perfect flower, a bird in flight, a person riding a bike past the school.
4. Groups meet to make a plan for taking their photos.
5. During the day, give the groups extra time to go outside and explore nature and activities in their surroundings.

On Day Two

6. Students view their photos and select five to ten to import into the multimedia software program of their choice.
7. Students arrange and rearrange the pictures on slides to decide on a story to tell.
8. Once the pictures are placed in an agreed upon order, student groups add captions, sounds, music, recorded narration, transitions and more to add pizzazz to the stories.
9. Groups share their presentations.

Engineering Extension: Biomimicry

Engineers use of the natural world as inspiration for design is called biomimicry. Biologically inspired designs include: air-going and sea-going vessels; navigation tools such as sonar and radar; medical imaging devices; biomedical technologies like prosthetics; and water and pollution treatment processes. Biomimicry has resulted in hundreds of creative products. Examples include: waterproof materials inspired by the slick leaves of the lotus plant whose very high water repellence washes away dirt particles each time it rains; Velcro which was invented as a result of a hiker using knowledge about the hook-and-loop system inspired by the prickly plant burrs that stick to our clothes; and the anti reflective screen that Intel modeled by observing the coating on a moth's eye, formed by bumps that stop light from reflecting on their eyes to keep predators from finding them. After learning about many real-life examples, student design engineers work in cooperative groups to create a new invention or improve an existing one, using the biomimicry of animals.

MATERIALS
Paper, pencils, markers, rulers
Internet access
Biomimicry Inventions Worksheet

PREPARE
1. During a class discussion, students list major categories of interest for design topics. Categories might include: Entertainment, Transportation, Fashion, Recreation, and Communication.
2. Have students come up with possible biomimicry ideas within each category by naming unique features of animals that could be used to inspire their designs. Ideas include:
   a. Entertainment – anti reflective screens modeled after a moth's eye
   b. Sports – running shoes using the mechanics of animals' feet
   c. Transportation – airplanes modeled after the shape of birds and their wings
   d. Fashion – competition swimsuits modeled after shark's skin
   e. Recreation – rock climbing using materials like the extremely sticky adhesive of a gecko's toes
   f. Medicine – artificial muscles modeled after natural structures like an elephant's trunk or an octopus's tentacle

DO
1. Students divide into cooperative interest groups by selecting a category from the list.
2. Each group searches the Internet to find out as much as they can about animal-inspired inventions in their category. Have them try to find drawings of the inventions and note the appearance of the original invention. How has it been modified or improved with time?
3. Students create a group invention and provide details using the Biomimicry Invention Worksheet.
4. Each group proudly presents its invention idea to the class.

Biomimicry Invention Worksheet

Write a description of your invention. Include the animal that inspired you and how the invention will make a difference to people in the category your group selected.

_____

_____

_____

_____

_____

Make a list of materials you will need to prototype your invention.

_____

_____

Draw or sketch your invention in the box below.

Math Extension: Nature Mastermind Game

Have students create and play Nature Mastermind to celebrate Children and Nature Awareness Month. Mastermind is a game of logic that became popular in the 1970s. Students use problem-solving strategies to discover the secret combination of objects their opponents have selected.

To prepare for the game, students collect items from nature. Start a few days before you plan to play the game so that you will have enough. Some of the items to collect may include: twigs, pebbles, leaves, petals, seeds and blades of grass. Make sure that you have six piles of nature items, so that each student places four or more of the same item in a baggie. Each student will have six baggies, identical to every other student in the class. To play the game, pairs of students each use six baggies with identical objects.

Directions for Game Play

1. One player becomes the code maker; the other becomes the code breaker. The code maker chooses a pattern of four single items selected from their six baggies and places them shielded from view. The goal is for the code breaker to duplicate the same objects and the same position as the code maker.

2. The code breaker tries to guess the pattern by placing four items from their six baggies. The code maker provides feedback by telling how many objects are correctly matched in both object and position and which have matching objects placed in the wrong position. For example, "of your four items, you have two correctly matched and only one is in the correct position."

3. After the feedback is provided the code breaker attempts another guess. Again the code maker provides feedback. The code breaker uses the feedback to deduce his next move. The game is over when the code is broken or ten attempts have elapsed.

4. After the class understands the game, have pairs of students play. Once they are proficient with the game, make the game more challenging by having the code makers select duplicate items from the same baggie as part of the four that make up the code.

Poetry Lesson for
Children and Nature Awareness Month:
The Gladness of Nature

In his poem *The Gladness of Nature*, William Cullen Bryant takes us on a nature trip and delights us with the gifts that nature gives. Through his sensitive ears and descriptive writing, children will hear: "… notes of joy from the hang-bird and wren, /And the gossip of swallows through all the sky." In this lesson, students personify nature.

MATERIALS
- William Cullen Bryant Biography and his poem *The Gladness of Nature*
- Word processing or desktop publishing software or pencils, pens and paper

PLAN
- Read and discuss William Cullen Bryan's biography and poem.
- Discuss the poem with the following questions:
  - What does Bryant mean by "Is this a time to be cloudy and sad?"
  - What does Bryant see in nature?
  - What interesting descriptive words does he use?
  - Where is personification used in the poem?

DO
Getting Ready to Write
- The poet begins his poem with the words "Is this a time to be cloudy and sad."
  Exchange the words *cloud* and *sad* with other synonyms.
  For example, *Is this a time to be angry and mean? or Is this a time to be frowning and crying?*
- List elements in nature they can use in their poems.
- How would they use personification to describe these elements reaction to nature?
  For example, *dancing clouds, singing birds, smiling fruits and flowers*

Writing the Poem
Using *The Gladness of Nature* as a model, students write poems of their own. Encourage line breaks so that the poem looks like a poem and not like a story.
- Begin with "Is this a time to be" and continue with the question students would ask.
- Continue the poem with "When" and describe an element in nature and what it is doing on such a beautiful day. Encourage personification.
- Continue the poem with other elements in nature and describe what each one does.

Editing and Publishing
- Students read and edit poems with partners.
- Have students use watercolors to paint a scene illustrating their poem.
- When painting dries thoroughly, write a part of their poem or their entire poem on the watercolor.

William Cullen Bryant Biography
November 3, 1794 – June 12, 1878

William Cullen Bryant was born a log cabin in Cummington, Massachusetts. His mother's family came to America on the Mayflower. His father's family came to the American colonies about twelve years later. His father was a physician and also a state legislator. His home in Massachusetts is now a museum.

William's father had a strong influence on him. William learned English poetry at a young age in his father's large personal library. Bryant's father encouraged William's writing, at times even sending William's poems to magazines for publication without his knowledge. At the age of ten, William had his first poem published and at thirteen had his first book of poetry published. He loved nature and celebrated it in his poems.

William studied law in Massachusetts and at twenty-one he passed the bar and became a lawyer. He would walk seven miles to work every day. On these walks, he was moved by the nature he observed. His love of nature would be celebrated in his poems. Although his first love was poetry, the life of a poet was not practical for him. But his literary dreams would be fulfilled in journalism. He moved his family to New York City and began his career as editor-in-chief of the New York Evening Post, one of the nation's most respected newspapers. He wrote articles, essays and poems that defended human rights, free trade, Abraham Lincoln, and the abolition of slavery. His influence helped the establishment of Central Park and the Metropolitan Museum of Art. He held the position of editor-in-chief until his death.

In his lifetime, he didn't publish many poems but he was very popular due to his writing as a journalist, and his many public speeches where he spoke about his views. Bryant was one of the founders of the Republican Party, and at one time he even thought about running for President of the United States. In New York City in Manhattan there is a square named Bryant Park to honor him.

The Gladness of Nature
by William Cullen Bryant

Is this a time to be cloudy and sad,
When our mother Nature laughs around;
When even the deep blue heavens look glad,
And gladness breathes from the blossoming ground?

There are notes of joy from the hang-bird and wren,
And the gossip of swallows through all the sky;
The ground-squirrel gaily chirps by his den,
And the wilding bee hums merrily by.

The clouds are at play in the azure space,
And their shadows at play on the bright green vale,
And here they stretch to the frolic chase,
And there they roll on the easy gale.

There's a dance of leaves in that aspen bower,
There's a titter of winds in that beechen tree,
There's a smile on the fruit, and a smile on the flower,
And a laugh from the brook that runs to the sea.

And look at the broad-faced sun, how he smiles
On the dewy earth that smiles in his ray,
On the leaping waters and gay young isles;
Ay, look, and he'll smile thy gloom away.

Additional Poems for Children and Nature Awareness Month

The Swing by Robert Louis Stevenson is one of his many famous poems. Children of all ages can identify with the feeling of going up in a swing. How beautiful the sight must be on a spring day in an English countryside – beautiful enough to want to capture it in watercolors.

In this lesson, students will research an English watercolorist. Here are a few to get you started: Elizabeth Allingham, Elizabeth Blackadder, Sandra Blow, Mildred Ann Butler, John Sell Cotman, David Cox, Joshua Cristall, Copley Fielding, Miles Birkett Foster, Samuel Palmer, Peter de Wint and John Varley. Select an artist, learn something about the artist and paint a countryside watercolor in their style.

The Swing
from *A Child's Garden of Verses*
by Robert Louis Stevenson

How do you like to go up in a swing,
Up in the air so blue?
Oh, I do think it the pleasantest thing
Ever a child can do!
Up in the air and over the wall,
Till I can see so wide,
River and trees and cattle and all
Over the countryside—
Till I look down on the garden green,
Down on the roof so brown—
Up in the air I go flying again,
Up in the air and down!

In the poem, *There Was a Child Went Forth*, Walt Whitman writes about children's experiences with nature. These sensory memories remain with them forever. Walt Whitman is known as the father of free verse. Free verse follows the natural rhythms of speech and does not rhyme. In Whitman's travels as a journalist in America he met many people. Whitman believed that poetry should reflect the many voices of America. His poetry mimicked natural speech. How would this poem differ if it were written in rhyme rather than free verse? Have students pick their favorite stanza and write it as a rhyme.

There Was a Child Went Forth
by Walt Whitman

There was a child went forth every day.
And the first object he look'd upon, that object he became,
And that object became part of him for the day, or a certain part of the day,
Or for many years or stretching cycles of years.
The early lilacs became part of this child,
And grass, and white and red morning-glories, and white and red clover, and
the song of the phoebe-bird,
And the Third-month lambs, and the sow's pink-faint litter, and the mare's
foal, and the cow's calf,
And the noisy brood of the barn-yard, or by the mire of the pondside,
And the fish suspending themselves so curiously below there, and the
beautiful curious liquid,
And the water-plants with their graceful flat heads, all became part of him.
The field-sprouts of Fourth-month and Fifth-month became part of him,
Winter-grain sprouts, and those of the light-yellow corn, and the esculent roots
of the garden,
And the apple-trees cover'd with blossoms, and the fruit afterward, and
wood-berries, and the commonest weeds by the road,
And the oldest drunkard staggering home from the out-house of the tavern
whence he had lately risen,
And the schoolmistress that pass'd on her way to the school
And the friendly boys that pass'd and the quarrelsome boys,
And the tidy and fresh-cheek'd girls, and the barefoot negro boy and girl,
And all the changes of city and country wherever he went.

His own parents, he that had father'd him and she that had conceiv'd him in
her womb and birth'd him.
They gave this child more of themselves than that,
They gave him afterward every day, they became part of him.
The mother at home quietly placing the dishes on the supper-table, 22

The mother with mild words, clean her cap and gown, a wholesome odor
    falling off her person and clothes as she walks by,
The father, strong, self-sufficient, manly, mean, anger'd, unjust,
The blow, the quick loud word, the tight bargain, the crafty lure,
The family usages, the language, the company, the furniture, the yearning
    and swelling heart,
Affection that will not be gainsay'd, the sense of what is real, the thought if
    after all it should prove unreal,
The doubts of day-time and the doubts of night-time, the curious whether
    and how,
Whether that which appears so is so, or is it all flashes and specks?
Men and women crowding fast in the streets, and if they are not flashes and
    specks, what are they?
The streets themselves and the facades of houses and goods in the windows
Vehicles, teams, the heavy-plank'd wharves, the huge crossing at the
    ferries,
The village on the highland seen from afar at sunset, the river between,
Shadows, aureola and mist, the light falling on the roofs and gables of
    white or brown two miles off,
The schooner nearby sleepily dropping down the tide, the little boat slack-
    tow'd astern,
The hurrying tumbling waves, quick-broken crests, slapping,
The strata of color'd clouds, the long bar or maroon-tint away solitary by
    itself, the spread of purity it lies motionless in,
The horizon's edge, the flying sea-crow, the fragrance of salt marsh and
    shore mud,
These became part of that child who went forth every day, and who now
    goes, and will always go forth every day.

April – Earth Day Lessons and Projects
Technology Lesson for Earth Day: Earth Day Public Service Announcements (PSAs)

In this lesson, student groups create a public service announcement (PSA) that demonstrates ways in which the planet can be a healthier place for all living things. Students use presentation software to create their PSA and export into a movie format.

MATERIALS
- Internet access
- Multimedia presentation software such as PowerPoint, HyperStudio, Keynote or Google Docs
- Drawing software such as Kid Pix, Tux Paint or Sketchpad
- Photo editors such as Photoshop Elements, PIXLR (a free on-line photo editor)
- Storyboard planning worksheet, two copies per group
- Pencils and other drawing tools

PLAN
Students produce a PSA for Earth Day to inform their audience of ways to keep the planet safe. A PSA is similar to a commercial. The difference is that a PSA persuades viewers to adopt their point of view while commercials encourage them to buy a product.

Brainstorm a class list of Earth Day topics that can be the subject of the Earth Day PSA.
- Some possible topics include:
    - Energy
    - Water
    - Paper
    - Clean air
    - Recycling
    - Natural resources
- Using the list, discuss possible things to include in the presentation. Some suggestions are:
    - Create and record an Earth Day pledge.
    - Photograph or video an endangered habitat in the neighborhood.
    - Interview others (students, parents, faculty, experts, etc.).
    - Include links to Earth Day Internet sites.
    - Present the history of Earth Day.
    - Produce original drawings.
    - Add additional class ideas.

DO

Student groups design and produce a multimedia Earth Day PSA following the steps below.

- Search the Internet for information, pictures, videos, recordings, and so on to use.
- Use the PSA Storyboard Worksheet to plan the production.
- Open a new document in the software program to be used.
- Construct slide shows to have at least five frames and last no longer than three minutes.
- Select layout, color scheme, text styles, graphics, multimedia from the Internet and other features to include.
- Add text boxes, graphics, illustrations, sounds, videos and links.
- Play, review, revise and fine tune the production.
- Present the finished multimedia project to other classmates, schoolmates, family, and so on.

Import your PSA into movie-making software like iMovie to add more features. In iMovie you can change the look of your video and add slow or fast motion. We Video is another option for Chrome users that produces the same results. We Video is a cloud-based, collaborative video and creation platform. You may wish to combine all PSAs into one larger class presentation.

PSA Storyboard Planning Worksheet

Slide # Dialogue/Narration Audio Effects/Graphics Videos/Links Transition	Slide # Dialogue/Narration Audio Effects/Graphics Videos/Links Transition
Slide # Dialogue/Narration Audio Effects/Graphics Videos/Links Transition	Slide # Dialogue/Narration Audio Effects/Graphics Videos/Links Transition

Earth Day Extensions

Science Extension:
Shades of Ozone – Some Good, Some Bad

In springtime as warmer weather arrives, the amount of ozone in the air often increases. In this lesson students learn about the benefits of good ozone and the harm that bad ozone causes. Students will place specially-prepared paper strips in different locations around the school to find where bad ozone tends to hang out. After collecting and testing the strips, students will record their data. For classrooms that plan to create a visual presentation or a written notebook, record procedural steps with digital photographs. Prepare a map of your schoolyard so that you can determine where your samples are placed.

1. During a class discussion encourage students to expand on the following ozone facts:
    a. Ozone is a molecule that is made of gaseous elements.
    b. Good ozone exists in the stratosphere and makes it possible for us to be outside without being harmed. It protects life on earth from the sun's ultraviolet rays.
    c. Bad ozone is found much closer to the earth and exists in the lower level of the atmosphere known as the troposphere. The ozone in the troposphere is an air pollutant that causes damage to human health, vegetation and many common materials.
    d. The levels of ozone in the troposphere vary and are worse on warm days.
    e. Some causes of bad ozone are automobile exhaust, gasoline vapor, fossil fuel, power and plant emissions.
2. The class will be working with ozone test strips. The strips can easily be purchased online through Amazon.com or can be made using the directions in the Making Schoenbein Ozone Test Strips section of this extension lesson.
3. Divide the class into small groups of three or four students. Distribute tape, ozone test strips, and a spray bottle filled with distilled water to each group.
4. Have students place some test strips in the classroom and some strips outside to find the locations that have the highest ozone layers. This is best done on a warm sunny day. Instruct students to select spots to place the strips where they won't be in direct sunlight or disturbed for several hours. Begin as early in the school day as possible and leave them in place until the end of the day.
5. As they place each strip, have students spray the strip with the distilled water. Hang the strip in the test area with tape.
6. Distribute self-sealing plastic bags and black markers when it's time to collect the strips. Students will use the marker to note where they found each strip. As they collect each strip, place each strip in a separate sealable plastic bag.
7. Have students spray the collected strips generously with the distilled water. Observe the color to determine the amount of ground level ozone based on the Schoenbein color scale. The scale ranges from no color for the least amount of ozone to blue or purple for the most. A lavender hue would be a mid-level ozone result.
8. Have students discuss and record any changes in the test paper they observe. Why do the test papers differ? Note that heavy traffic areas have high nitrogen oxide levels and may result in false positive readings. Research why humidity may be a factor in the test results.

9. Have each group write paragraphs describing the results of their tests. Create an Ozone Notebook and give an oral report of results to the class. Include maps of their observations and pictures taken with a digital camera.

Directions for Making Schoenbein Ozone Test Strips

This works well as a teacher demonstration with students recording in their notebooks the materials and the steps to follow. Iodide is on many hazardous substances list and check your local regulations prior to working with it in the classroom. Use gloves and eye protection when working with iodide.

Schoenbein test strips were first developed by Christian Friedrich Schoenbein in 1839 in Switzerland. He mixed starch, potassium iodide and distilled water spread on filter paper to measure the ozone in the troposphere. Ozone causes iodide to oxidize into iodine staining the test strips a shade of purple. The more intense the color, the more ozone is present.

What You'll Need
- 1 teaspoon of potassium iodide
- Distilled water
- Filter paper or coffee filter paper
- Hot plate
- Corn starch
- Glass stirring rod
- Small brush
- 8.4 oz. glass beaker or other glass container
- Microwave safe glass plate
- Hot pad or mitt for removing the beaker from the heat source
- Scissors
- Air tight plastic bag or container

Directions
a. Put 3.4 ounces of distilled water into the glass beaker or container and add 1 1/4 teaspoons cornstarch.
b. Use a hot plate or other heat device to heat the mixture.
c. Stir with the glass rod while heating until the mixture thickens and becomes clear or translucent.
d. Remove the container from the heat and cool.
e. Stir in 1/4 teaspoon of the potassium iodide.
f. Let the mixture cool until it thickens into a paste.
g. Open a coffee filter paper and place it on the glass plate.
h. Carefully brush the paste evenly onto both sides of the filter paper.
i. Cut the paper into 1-inch wide strips.
j. Place the plate in a microwave oven for about 45 seconds or in a conventional oven on a low setting to completely dry the paper.
k. Place the strips in the plastic bag or food container.
l. Store them in a dark place.

Engineering Extension: Green Spaces

Industrial engineering is a relatively new profession. For the past several years more than half of the world's population has lived in cities. As more and more people move into cities, the focus has centered on designing "livable" cities. The best of these are known as much for their open and green spaces as they are for their buildings and culture. In this lesson students do the job of industrial engineers as they walk around the neighborhood surrounding the school and evaluate the area's green and open spaces.

Tell the class that they will be taking the role of industrial engineers to evaluate their school neighborhood on a walk in which they look for green and open spaces. As they walk, they sketch and describe sites that are a benefit to the community and those that are a liability. Have the class make a list of possible green and open spaces they might find on their walk. Write the list on the board or a chart. This list could include:

- Parks
- Community gardens
- Cemeteries
- Playgrounds
- Public seating areas
- Plazas
- Vacant lots
- Parkways and alleyways

Discuss what type of sites might benefit the community by helping to enhance the beauty and environmental quality of life in the neighborhood. What sites might detract from the community? Are there areas where trash has not been picked up? Are there sites without public access? Are there rows of houses or buildings without green space?

Divide students into small groups. Distribute clipboards, pencils and two or three sheets of the Green Spaces Chart to each student. Have the groups walk several blocks around the school accompanied by adult volunteers. As they walk, have them look for open and green spaces that enhance or detract from the beauty and livability of the community. Use the Green Spaces Chart for sketching what they see, describing the location of the site and describing why the site is either a benefit or liability to the community.

Students become industrial engineers as they work in groups to make a plan based on their findings. Groups begin by discussing their completed charts. The groups then create a plan that adds additional green space, more areas for the public to enjoy and mitigates the liabilities that they have encountered.

Green Spaces Chart

Draw a sketch of the green and open spaces you see on your walk. Describe the location of your site by giving details that would help others find it. Either describe it as a community asset or a community liability.

Sketch of the Site	Description of the Location	Describe Community Benefit	Describe Community Liability

Math Extension:
Reusing Old Math Textbooks –
May the Forest Be With You

Paper is a major contributor to waste landfills. Every year many old textbooks are thrown out. Your school probably has a stack of old math textbooks that will work well for this activity. Your students will feel a great sense of accomplishment as they work through these fun directions. Have your students create their own list of directions to further extend learning. Write the steps on a board or a chart.

1. Open the textbook to a random page and write the page number.
2. Open to a new page and write that number.
   a. Add both numbers together to find the sum.
   b. Subtract to find the difference.
   c. Multiply the numbers to find the quotient.
3. Open your textbook to the last numbered page.
   a. Round the page number to nearest tenth.
   b. Round the page number to the nearest one hundredth.
4. Write and solve the last problem on the first three odd numbered pages.
5. Write and solve the first problem on the last four even numbered page.
6. Write a one-digit page number and a two-digit page number. Use them to create and solve a division problem.
7. Open your math book to a new random page and write the page number.
8. Open to another page and write that number.
   a. Use both numbers to create a fraction with the smallest number as the numerator and the largest number as the denominator.
   b. Reduce the fraction to its lowest terms.
9. Turn to a page near the end of the book and write the number on that page as a decimal.
   a. What number is in the hundreds place?
   b. What number is in the tens place?
   c. What number is in the ones place?
10. Write the title of your math book.
    a. How many vowels are in the title?
    b. How many consonants?
    c. Write the difference.
11. Use a ruler to measure your math book.
    a. How many inches wide is it?
    b. How many inches long is it?
    c. What is the area of your math book?

Poetry Lesson for Earth Day: The Cloud

Percy Bysshe Shelley was a Romantic poet. The Romantics admired and respected the untouched beauty of all that existed naturally on the earth. It was in nature that they wrote their powerful and majestic poetry. In Shelley's poem *The Cloud*, he describes the water cycle and the delicate balance of nature. Shelley would rejoice on Earth Day seeing that we are paying careful attention to the perfect balance that he admired and wrote about. In this lesson, students become an object in nature and write poems in the first person.

MATERIALS
- Percy Bysshe Shelley Biography and excerpt from his poem *The Cloud*
- Word processing or desktop publishing software or pencils, pens and paper

PLAN
- Read and discuss **Percy Bysshe Shelley**'s biography and poem.
- Discuss the poem with the following questions:
  - Where does Shelley use personification?
  - Why does Shelley use the word "I" when the cloud speaks?
  - What interesting verbs does Shelley use?
  - What does the cloud do to objects on the earth?
  - Why does the cloud "change but cannot die"?
  - Why does the cloud laugh "at my own cenotaph"?
  - How does the cloud seem like a magician?

DO
Getting Ready to Write
Using their imaginations, have students brainstorm to create a list of important natural forces they would want to become. For example: *rain, ocean, moon, sun*. As they give their responses list them on the board or on a chart and do the following:
- Have students pick a force from the list and describe how it affects aspects in nature.
- Encourage the use of personification. Refer to the poem for ideas.

Writing the Poem
- Begin the first line with "I" and follow with what their force does to nature.
- Continue writing about how their force affects nature.

Editing and Publishing
- Have students read and edit poems with partners.
- Have students illustrate their poems.
- Have students dramatically perform their poems using an appropriate voice.
- View videos of *The Cloud* on YouTube and create your own.

Percy Bysshe Shelley Biography
August 4, 1792 – July 8, 1822

Shelley was born in England. His father was a member of Parliament. He grew up in the countryside. In the meadows near his home, he enjoyed hunting and fishing. He was the oldest of seven children. He had a happy and imaginative childhood playing games that involved witches, wizards and demons.

At ten, he was sent to boarding school. He remained there for two years and then enrolled at Eton College. Within the first year at Eton, Shelley had two novels and two volumes of poetry published. He had an extremely difficult time at Eton. He was abused both physically and mentally, everyone bullying and making fun of him because of his eccentric ways. They called him "Mad Shelley." He had imagination and energy far beyond his physical strength. He loved to learn about magic and witchcraft and he could watch all night for ghosts. His interests were not like most of the other students who loved popular games. He did, however, enjoy boating and shooting. In the classroom, he was a Latin scholar. He loved to read and was also interested in science. During vacations back home, he was always telling his sisters tales of supernatural wonders.

At eighteen, Shelley enrolled at Oxford which seemed a better environment for him. After a few months there, Shelley was expelled from Oxford after publishing and distributing an essay *The Necessity of Atheism*. He went home to his angry parents. At nineteen, he went to Scotland with Harriet Westbrook and married. They separated and he began a relationship with Mary Godwin, who later wrote the novel *Frankenstein*. Eventually Harriet committed suicide leaving them free to marry.

From his childhood on, Shelley did not conform to the ideas of his society. As an adult, he believed that the changes proposed by the French Revolution would help society. He used his poetry to provoke a sense of revolution in people. He challenged authority in the way he lived, and was ostracized because of it. Shelley became one of the most well-loved and popular poets of his time. During his tumultuous life, he spent much of it thinking and appreciating nature, his work being an example of Romantic poetry. Shelley's imagination was constantly excited by the never-ending cycle of life that to him mirrored the human spirit. No poet has ever come closer to capturing in words the fullness of human emotion. After his death from drowning, Mary Shelley published a collection of his poetry and essays.

The Cloud

By Percy Bysshe Shelley

I bring fresh showers for the thirsting flowers,
    From the seas and the streams;
I bear light shade for the leaves when laid
    In their noonday dreams.
From my wings are shaken the dews that waken
    The sweet buds every one,
When rocked to rest on their mother's breast,
    As she dances about the sun.
I wield the flail of the lashing hail,
    And whiten the green plains under,
And then again I dissolve it in rain,
    And laugh as I pass in thunder.

I sift the snow on the mountains below,
    And their great pines groan aghast;
And all the night 'tis my pillow white,
    While I sleep in the arms of the blast.
Sublime on the towers of my skiey bowers,
    Lightning my pilot sits;
In a cavern under is fettered the thunder,
    It struggles and howls at fits;
Over earth and ocean, with gentle motion,
    This pilot is guiding me,
Lured by the love of the genii that move
    In the depths of the purple sea;
Over the rills, and the crags, and the hills,
    Over the lakes and the plains,
Wherever he dream, under mountain or stream,
    The Spirit he loves remains;
And I all the while bask in Heaven's blue smile,
    Whilst he is dissolving in rains.

The sanguine Sunrise, with his meteor eyes,
    And his burning plumes outspread,
Leaps on the back of my sailing rack,
    When the morning star shines dead;
As on the jag of a mountain crag,
    Which an earthquake rocks and swings,
An eagle alit one moment may sit
    In the light of its golden wings.
And when Sunset may breathe, from the lit sea beneath,
    Its ardours of rest and of love,
And the crimson pall of eve may fall
    From the depth of Heaven above,

With wings folded I rest, on mine aëry nest,
　　As still as a brooding dove.

That orbèd maiden with white fire laden,
　　Whom mortals call the Moon,
Glides glimmering o'er my fleece-like floor,
　　By the midnight breezes strewn;
And wherever the beat of her unseen feet,
　　Which only the angels hear,
May have broken the woof of my tent's thin roof,
　　The stars peep behind her and peer;
And I laugh to see them whirl and flee,
　　Like a swarm of golden bees,
When I widen the rent in my wind-built tent,
　　Till calm the rivers, lakes, and seas,
Like strips of the sky fallen through me on high,
　　Are each paved with the moon and these.

I bind the Sun's throne with a burning zone,
　　And the Moon's with a girdle of pearl;
The volcanoes are dim, and the stars reel and swim,
　　When the whirlwinds my banner unfurl.
From cape to cape, with a bridge-like shape,
　　Over a torrent sea,
Sunbeam-proof, I hang like a roof,
　　The mountains its columns be.
The triumphal arch through which I march
　　With hurricane, fire, and snow,
When the Powers of the air are chained to my chair,
　　Is the million-coloured bow;
The sphere-fire above its soft colours wove,
　　While the moist Earth was laughing below.

I am the daughter of Earth and Water,
　　And the nursling of the Sky;
I pass through the pores of the ocean and shores;
　　I change, but I cannot die.
For after the rain when with never a stain
　　The pavilion of Heaven is bare,
And the winds and sunbeams with their convex gleams
　　Build up the blue dome of air,
I silently laugh at my own cenotaph,
　　And out of the caverns of rain,
Like a child from the womb, like a ghost from the tomb,
　　I arise and unbuild it again.

Additional Poem for Earth Day

Ralph Waldo Emerson was born in Boston, Massachusetts in the early 19th century. In his poem, *Blight*, Emerson writes about the dangers imposed on our earth by "pirates of the universe." After reading and discussing the poem, students write a letter to Emerson describing what kids are doing on Earth Day to improve the environment.

Blight
by Ralph Waldo Emerson

Give me truths,
For I am weary of the surfaces,
And die of inanition. If I knew
Only the herbs and simples of the wood,…
And rare and virtuous roots, which in these woods
Draw untold juices from the common earth,
Untold, unknown, and I could surely spell
Their fragrance, and their chemistry apply
By sweet affinities to human flesh,
Driving the foe and stablishing the friend,—
O that were much, and I could be a part
Of the round day, related to the sun,
And planted world, and full executor
Of their imperfect functions.

But these young scholars who invade our hills,
Bold as the engineer who fells the wood,
And travelling often in the cut he makes,
Love not the flower they pluck, and know it not,
And all their botany is Latin names.
The old men studied magic in the flower,
And human fortunes in astronomy,
And an omnipotence in chemistry,
Preferring things to names, for these were men,
Were unitarians of the united world,
And wheresoever their clear eyebeams fell,
They caught the footsteps of the SAME. Our eyes
Are armed, but we are strangers to the stars,

Even in the hot pursuit of the best aims
And strangers to the mystic beast and bird,
And strangers to the plant and to the mine;
The injured elements say, Not in us;
And night and day, ocean and continent,
Fire, plant, and mineral say, Not in us,
And haughtily return us stare for stare.
For we invade them impiously for gain,
We devastate them unreligiously,
And coldly ask their pottage, not their love,
Therefore they shove us from them, yield to us
Only what to our griping toil is due;
But the sweet affluence of love and song,
The rich results of the divine consents
Of man and earth, of world beloved and lover,
The nectar and ambrosia are withheld;
And in the midst of spoils and slaves, we thieves
And pirates of the universe, shut out
Daily to a more thin and outward rind,
Turn pale and starve. Therefore to our sick eyes,
The stunted trees look sick, the summer short,
Clouds shade the sun, which will not tan our hay.
And nothing thrives to reach its natural term,
And life, shorn of its venerable length,
Even at its greatest space, is a defeat,
And dies in anger that it was a dupe,
And, in its highest noon and wantonness,
Is early frugal like a beggar's child:
With most unhandsome calculation taught,
Even in the hot pursuit of the best aims
And prizes of ambition, checks its hand,
Like Alpine cataracts, frozen as they leaped,
Chilled with a miserly comparison
Of the toy's purchase with the length of life.

April Engineering Lessons and Projects for Poetry Month: Drinking Straw Bands

Students become both pipers and engineers as they transform ordinary drinking straws into reed instruments to play in drinking straw bands. Students work in groups to modify straws of several shapes, lengths and widths. The bands perform their songs along with the poems they write later in this unit.

MATERIALS
- Drinking straws of all sizes and shapes – flexible, twistable, wide, narrow, long, short
- Scissors, tape and hole punch
- Photos of woodwind instruments

PLAN
- Discuss students' prior knowledge of woodwind instruments.
    - Create a list of woodwind instruments with the class.
    - Find out if any students have played or listened to one or more of the following or their variations: piccolo, flute, clarinet, oboe, recorder, saxophone, bassoon and English horn.
- Share pictures of woodwinds. The shape and size of the instrument determines the pitch of the notes. The smaller and shorter the instrument, the higher the pitch and the softer the sound. Use the pictures to compare the similarities and differences between and among woodwind instruments. For example, a piccolo produces a higher pitch note than a flute.
- To make music from a woodwind instrument, a musician blows air into the mouthpiece and makes notes by covering holes on the tube.
- Conduct a class demonstration on how to create a woodwind instrument as follows:
    - Distribute one straight medium-length straw and scissors to each student.
    - Show students how they can effectively flatten one end of a straw by biting it with their teeth and squeezing the ends between their fingers.
    - Students cut the flattened end of the straw into a point.
    - When the point is cut, have them flatten the end again.
    - Have them blow into the mouthpiece to produce the new instrument's sound.
    - Repeat by cutting the straw instrument in half and notice the change in the sound.

DO
- Divide the class into small groups.
- Distribute straws of various shapes and sizes, tape, and hole punches to each group.
- Tell students they will have twenty minutes to modify the straw instruments to add various pitches and notes with the purpose of producing a song.
- Allow additional time for a dress rehearsal. Make any straw modifications as necessary.
- Have each group perform their song.
- Record the performances.

Poetry Month STEM Extensions

Science Extension:
Catalog Poetry Weather and Climate

Students will write a catalog poem after learning the difference between climate and weather. Using the Climate/Weather handout that shows a sample weather report and a sample climate description for Anchorage, Alaska, students will have a springboard for their catalog poem.

Through discussion, questioning and studying the handout help students discover that weather is always changing and is reported everyday while climate is the average weather in a place occurring over a long period of time. People making short-term decisions on what to wear or a good activity for next weekend would use a weather report. When planning a future skiing or surfing vacation, a climate map would be more useful.

Students use the Anchorage Weather Forecast to decide what clothes they would wear and what activities they would plan on the days reported. They use the Anchorage Climate Averages to decide when they would like to visit Anchorage and why.

Students use the weather information they discussed to compile a list of weather and climate words. They use the words and ideas to compose catalog poems, also known as list poems. These poems are different than prose. To write them, students focus on making them poetic by concentrating on organization, word choice, phrasing and rhythm. The poet decides whether to rhyme or not to rhyme the words in a catalog poem.

Follow the directions below to write a class weather catalog poem.
1. Select a weather word such as wind, rain, sun, lightning or thunder as the subject.
2. Begin the poem with the word selected.
3. Brainstorm to create a list of all the words and phrases the subject brings to mind.
4. Encourage students to use all their senses.
5. Students arrange the words and phrases to compose a class catalog poem.
6. Remind students to concentrate on organization, word choice, phrases and rhythm.

Using the class catalog poem as an example, have students work in pairs to create catalog poems of their own. Place the poems on a Poetry Month bulletin board. As an extension, have students create illustrations for their poems.

Weather Forecast
Anchorage, Alaska November 28 – 30, 2015

Saturday
11/28
36 | 29 °F

Saturday	40 % Precip. / 0 in

Showers early, then cloudy in the afternoon. Temps nearly steady in the mid 30s. Winds light and variable. Chance of rain 40%.

Saturday Night	20 % Precip. / 0 in

Cloudy skies. Low 29F. Winds light and variable.

Sunday
11/29
32 | 24 °F

Sunday	20 % Precip. / 0 in

Cloudy early with partial sunshine expected late. Temps nearly steady in the low to mid 30s. Winds light and variable.

Sunday Night	0 % Precip. / 0 in

Generally fair. Low 24F. Winds light and variable.

Monday
11/30
28 | 23 °F

Monday	10 % Precip. / 0 in

Partly cloudy skies. High 28F. Winds NNE at 5 to 10 mph.

Monday Night	10 % Precip. / 0 in

Overcast. Low 23F. Winds N at 5 to 10 mph.

Anchorage Climate Averages

Climate Alaska - Anchorage   °C | °F

	Jan	Feb	Mar	Apr	May	Jun
Average high in °F:	23	27	34	44	56	63
Average low in °F:	11	14	19	29	40	48
Av. precipitation in inch:	0.75	0.71	0.59	0.47	0.71	0.98
Days with precipitation:	7	6	7	4	5	7
Hours of sunshine:	78	114	210	254	268	288
Average snowfall in :	11	11	10	4	0	0

	Jul	Aug	Sep	Oct	Nov	Dec
Average high in °F:	65	64	55	40	28	25
Average low in °F:	52	50	42	29	17	13
Av. precipitation in inch:	1.81	3.27	2.99	2.05	1.14	1.1
Days with precipitation:	11	15	15	11	8	7
Hours of sunshine:	255	184	128	96	68	49
Average snowfall in :	0	0	0	8	13	17

Technology Extension:
Concrete Poems

In this technology extension lesson students will learn about and create Concrete Poems also known as Shape Poems. Students will become proficient at font usage, spacing, sizing and modifying. Students will also learn how to place a background picture behind text. To introduce concrete poetry to the class, do the following:.

1. Display the unfinished Flower Concrete Poem located on the following page on a board or chart.
2. Point out that in this concrete poem the words and letters are arranged within the flower parts. The final poem will take on the shape of the flower.
3. Discuss the parts of the poem that appear in the petals and the stamen.
4. Students complete the unfinished poem with new words that describe the flower and the feelings flowers inspire in people.
5. Write the words and letters in a variety of shapes and sizes, demonstrating how the placement of words is integral to the poem.
6. As students suggest words and phrases, arrange these within the outline of the shape.

When the class poem is complete, students work in pairs to create concrete poems at the computer as follows:
1. Student pairs search the Internet for the shape they want to use for their poem. Encourage them to select graphics that have easily recognizable forms such as geometric shapes, flowers or animals. Students can find many shapes by searching for coloring book images using Google.
2. Copy or drag and insert the shape into a word processing program and size it so that it can contain the words of their poem.
3. Using the text wrap feature of their word processing program, have students place the picture behind the text. You must place the image behind text in order to write over the image.
4. Remind students that in a concrete poem the picture their words form is as important as the poem.
5. Pairs write the poem within the outline of the shape they selected.
6. Size, shape and manipulate the words and letters appropriately to fill the shape.

CONCRETE POEM

Tantalizing
fragrantly delicious
Springtime delight
Like a painting
Beautiful colors
Spring arrived

Pollination
Petals, stigma, stamen style, every anther, filament
Petal -- parts of Natures Artwork
Flowers

BEES
LOVE YOUR
Sweet Nectar
and harvest honey
for my morning tea
Blowing in the breeze

Math Extension:
Oulipo Snowball Poems

The philosophy Oulipo (Ouvoir de Litterature Potentielle) is an acronym from French roughly translated as "the seeking of new structures and patterns which may be used by writers in any way they enjoy". Oulipo provides a connection between the study of poetry and mathematics. Developed by French scientists and mathematicians, Oulipo poetry is written within a system of structural constraints and is designed to produce endless outcomes. In this extension students will be introduced to a popular Oulipo exercise, the snowball poem. The snowball is a progressive poem. In this lesson students will build a progressive snowball poem that starts with a one-word sentence and builds up sequentially with each line containing one word more than the last.

After explaining what Oulipo means, explain that there are many popular exercises that use the philosophy of Oulipo. One of the most popular is the progressive snowball poem. Demonstrate how the construction of the poem works by creating one with the whole class. Place a one-word beginning on the board or chart. Have class members build the poem by adding lines that progressively have one more word than the next. Here is an example.

Flowers

Many colors

Arrival of spring

Blowing in the wind

Surrounded by bees and butterflies

Children have patiently waited for you

Your breathtaking fragrance fills the crisp air

Divide the class into small groups. Distribute chart paper and markers to each group. Groups choose a one-word noun to begin. Groups write additional lines as in the example. Set a goal of writing as many lines as possible within a twenty-minute time frame. At the end of twenty minutes, groups present their poems.

VARIATIONS

1. You can build on this foundation extension by constructing additional poems. There are many varieties of Oulip poetry exercises to choose from. For example, begin a snowball poem with one word on the first line. The second line is also one word, but with one additional letter. The lines grow progressively by making each line with a new word one letter longer than the previous word.

2. Another exercise is the S+7. In this exercise, writers replace each common noun in a poem with the common noun that follows it in a dictionary. For example, "To be, or not to be – that is the question . . ." becomes "To be, or not to be – that is the quetsal . . ." The word used to replace the noun varies with the dictionary used.

Poetry Lesson for Poetry Month: Introduction to Songs of Innocence

If William Blake were alive today, he would be the first to acknowledge the power and magic of poetry. In his poem, William Blake creates a magical world where his piper has the power to make the innocent child happy. First the Piper is: "Piping songs of pleasant glee." Next he sings "songs of happy cheer!" Finally, the piper writes his happy songs: "In a book, that all may read." This makes the poet's words eternal and accessible so that all children can experience the joy the Piper's words bring. In this lesson, students become the Piper and pipe a song that makes the listener happy.

MATERIALS
- William Blake's Biography and his poem *Introduction to Songs of Innocence*
- Word processing or desktop publishing software or pencils, pens and paper

PLAN
- Read and discuss William Blake's biography and poem.
- Discuss the poem with the following questions:
  - Where is the Piper in the beginning of the poem?
  - Why does the child want the piper to pipe a song?
  - What does the poet mean when he writes "he wept to hear"?

DO
Getting Ready to Write
- Using their imaginations, students brainstorm the following questions as if they were the Piper. As the students gives their responses, list them on the board or on a chart.
  - What will they be doing and where will they be at the beginning of the poem?
    For **example**: *sitting in a cloud, sitting by the ocean, walking in the meadow, lying in the garden,*.
  - Who will ask them to pipe a song?
    For **example**: *my grandmother, my mother, my uncle or my brother.*
  - What will they ask them to pipe about?
    For **example**: *the river, the mountains,* or *the sun.*
  - How will they expand their responses?
    For **example**: *the river's water splashes calmly, the mountains touch the clouds* or *the sun warmly smiles on me.*

Writing the Poem
- Students write poems of their own referring to the brainstormed list on the board. You may wish to begin by writing a class poem together.
  - Begin the poem with where they are and what they are doing.
  - Continue by telling who will ask them to pipe a song.
  - Suggest they continue writing their poems creating a peaceful and beautiful world by describing places in nature that make it that way.

Editing and Publishing
- Students read and edit poems with a partner.
- William Blake often framed his poetry with borders. Look at some of his border designs and give your poem a beautiful border.

William Blake Biography
November 28, 1757 – August 12, 1827

William Blake was born in Soho, England. His father was haberdasher and hosier. They had seven children. His parents always supported his genius. When he was only four years old, he began to have visions. In one, he saw a tree filled with angels who sang and waved their wings in the branches. These visions were to become the subjects of his drawings and poetry throughout his life.

William's love of drawing and writing began at a very young age. Although he never attended school, his mother taught him to read. When he was ten, his father, recognizing his artistic talent, sent him to drawing school. There he learned to develop his skills by copying prints in drawing books. His teacher at the school sent him to Westminster Abbey, a famous church in London. At the Abbey, he spent his time sketching the statues. These statues were a major influence on his drawings. He was admitted to the Royal Academy Schools as an engraver where he began to exhibit his work.

When William was 25, he married Catherine Butcher. When they married, Catherine could not read or write. William became her teacher. They had a happy marriage and remained together until his death.

As a teenager, he started writing poetry and combining his writing with his drawings and engravings. Much of his poetry was written about the conditions in British cities. These cities were unsanitary and overcrowded. As he walked along the streets of London, he saw children being mistreated and working very long hours in city factories. There was discontent among the working classes. In his visions, he saw a different world. He saw angels dancing around the sun that shined over London and children laughing on clouds. He wrote about the innocence of children. Much of his artistic energy was used to bring about a change in the way people behaved towards children. In this spirit, he wrote *Introduction to Songs of Innocence*.

Introduction to Songs of Innocence

by William Blake

Piping down the valleys wild,
Piping songs of pleasant glee,
On a cloud I saw a child,
And he laughing said to me:

"Pipe a song about a Lamb!"
So I piped with merry cheer.
"Piper, pipe that song again;"
So I piped: he wept to hear.

"Drop thy pipe, thy happy pipe;
Sing thy songs of happy cheer!"
So I sung the same again,
While he wept with joy to hear.

"Piper, sit thee down and write
In a book, that all may read."
So he vanish'd from my sight,
And I pluck'd a hollow reed.

And I made a rural pen,
And I stained the water clear,
And I wrote my happy songs
Every child may joy to hear.

Additional Poems for Poetry Month

In her poem *Poetry*, Dame Edith Louisa Sitwell writes that poetry has the power to unveil "the meaning of all things." In this lesson, students observe a simple object such as a rock, a leaf and so on to discover the secrets that it holds. Afterwards, they write a poem about the secrets their object unveils to them.

Poetry
by Dame Edith Louisa Sitwell

Ennobles the heart and the eyes,
and unveils the meaning of all things
upon which the heart and the eyes dwell.
It discovers the secret rays of the universe,
and restores to us forgotten paradises.

In his poem *Poetry*, James McIntyer writes that poetry exists in all things, in for example, the motion of ships "sailing o'er the ocean." Have students write a short essay supporting or disputing McIntyer's view that poetry exists in all things.

Poetry
by James McIntyre

Poetry to us is given
As stars beautify the heaven,
Or, as the sunbeams when they gleam,
Sparkling so bright upon the stream;
And the poetry of motion
Is ship sailing o'er the ocean
Or, when the bird doth graceful fly,
Seeming to float upon the sky;
For poetry is the pure cream
And essence of the common theme.

Poetic thoughts the mind doth fill,
When on broad plain to view a hill;
On barren heath how it doth cheer
To see in distance herd of deer.
And poetry breathes in each flower
Nourished by the gentle shower,
In song of birds upon the trees
And humming of busy bees.
'Tis solace for the ills of life,
A soothing of the jars and strife;
For poets feel it a duty
To sing of both worth and beauty

April Math Lessons and Projects for Math Awareness Month:
Math in the Real World Scavenger Hunt

In this lesson, students work in groups in a real-world math scavenger hunt using newspapers and magazines. Working from a handout, teams search for items that depict how math exists in their daily lives. As sample items are found they are placed on a project board.

MATERIALS
- Newspapers
- Magazines
- Math in the Real-World Scavenger Hunt Worksheet
- Poster paper or poster boards
- Scissors
- Glue, paste, tape

PLAN
- Students bring newspapers and magazines in advance.
- Discuss the sections of a daily newspaper and the format of some sample magazines.
- Distribute the Real-World Scavenger Hunt Worksheet.
- Discuss where some of the items would be found in the sections of a daily newspaper or in magazines.

DO
- Students work in pairs to find items from the list, and place their found artifacts on poster paper or poster boards.
- In the specified time, students find as many of the twenty items as they can and number the items on the poster board to match the list on the worksheet.
- Early finishers, add to the list and to their project boards.
- Finished posters will be presented to the class and displayed in the classroom.
- Alternatively, the Internet could be used for this activity; however, it requires a networked printer and a lot of paper.

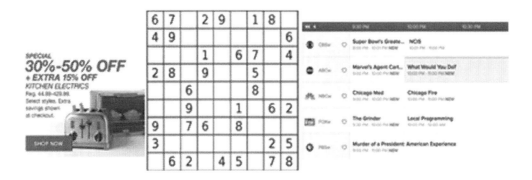

Math in the Real-World Scavenger Hunt Handout

1. Classified ad for a job that requires good math skills
2. Ad that includes a telephone number, fax number and/or Internet address
3. Item of clothing with a two-digit number
4. Product reduced 50% or more
5. A business logo with a geometric shape
6. Item that costs more than $1500
7. Ad that tells or shows how much money you can save
8. Sudoku or other number puzzle
9. Picture of an item of clothing with parallel lines
10. Ad that illustrates identical items
11. Something that lists miles per gallon
12. Comic strip or cartoon that relates to math in the real world
13. Listing of the time and date(s) of an event
14. Measurement of an item (weight, length, etc.)
15. Real estate listing for property over one million dollars
16. A bar, circle, or line graph
17. Television or movie schedule showing time or date
18. Current mortgage or interest rates
19. A picture of a consumer using math in the real world
20. Ad that shows a monthly payment amount

Math Awareness Month STEM Extension Lessons

Science Extension:
Calorie Cavalcade

In this extension students will be introduced to calories. They will learn what they are and how the body uses them. Discuss the information below:

1. A calorie is the amount of heat required to raise the temperature of a gram of water 1 degree Celsius or 1.8 degrees Fahrenheit.
2. Calories in foods provide us with energy.
3. The foods we eat are composed of carbohydrates, proteins and fats.
4. Carbohydrates and proteins have four calories per gram and a gram of fat has nine calories.
5. When we eat more calories than we burn, our body stores them as fat and we gain weight.
6. The daily optimum calories people need is generally between 1800 and 2200 calories but varies according to age, body type, activity level and gender.
7. All human activities require energy.
8. We need energy for our heart to beat and our lungs to breath.
9. We burn calories even when we are sitting, watching TV, or reading a book.

Students work with partners and do the following to complete the Calorie Cavalcade Handout:

1. List ten foods they typically eat in a day.
2. Use an Internet capable device to determine the calories for each item on their list.
3. Record the calories on the worksheet.

Helpful Websites

The calorie-counter websites listed below provide easy access to needed information.
   https://www.fitwatch.com/caloriecounter
   http://www.newcaloriecounter.com/articles/goverment/usda/usda_national_nutrient_database_for_standard_reference.html

Once students have completed listing the foods and calories, they answer the questions on the handout. To conclude the lesson, students write a report telling what they have learned about calories and how it will influence their choice of food and exercise in the future.

Calorie Cavalcade Handout

FOOD		CALORIES
1.		
2.		
3.		
4.		
5.		
6.		
7.		
8.		
9.		
10.		

1. What surprises you about the calories in some of your typical food choices?

_____

_____

2. What items on your list have the most and least amount of calories?

_____

_____

3. Check the activities you do for at least one hour once a week. Note the approximate calories burned. The calories below are for children ages 9 to 14 according to parenthood.com.

_____Riding a bike – 130 calories   _____Skateboarding – 160 calories

_____Watching T.V. – 22 calories   _____Doing homework – 39 calories

_____Playing video games – 32 calories   _____Walking – 198 calories

_____Dancing – 190 calories   _____Swimming – 195 calories

_____Playing Hopscotch – 170 calories   _____Playing Frisbee – 100 calories

_____Sleeping, reading or sitting still – 35 calories   _____Other _____

Technology Extension: Tantalizing Tangrams

Tangrams are ancient Chinese puzzles that use seven pieces to make shapes, patterns, and pictures. They belong to a group of puzzles known as dissection puzzles. In these puzzles one shape is cut into defined pieces that are used to make new shapes. A tangram begins as a square. The seven pieces include: two large right triangles, one medium-sized right triangle, two small right triangles, one small square and one parallelogram. Working with tangrams is a great way to increase geometry skills, practice spatial relations and improve creative thinking.

In this math-based technology lesson, students follow the directions on the Make a Tangram Handout to create their tangrams. After cutting the pieces as shown in the directions, students create a table in a word processing program to show how many of the seven tangram pieces they use to make each shape. To make the table have students do the following:

1. Create a table in a word processing program that has eight columns and seven rows.
2. Merge columns two through eight in row one and write "NUMBER OF PIECES" in the merged column.
3. Write the word "SHAPES" in row two, column one.
4. Write the numbers one through seven sequentially in the remaining columns of row two.
5. Write the words Square, Triangle, Rectangle, Trapezoid and Parallelogram sequentially in column one, rows three through seven.
6. Save the table as "Tangram Shapes Chart."

Divide students into pairs and have them find and record the number of pieces they can use to make each shape in the chart. Here is an example chart with a few of the answers recorded:

SHAPES	NUMBER OF PIECES						
	1	2	3	4	5	6	7
Square	yes	yes	no	no	no	no	yes
Triangle							
Rectangle							
Trapezoid							
Parallelogram							

Further Exploration

Follow up by experimenting with the tangram pieces. Arranged correctly, using all seven pieces, you can make a large rectangle or triangle as well as a square. Try using all seven pattern pieces to make pictures of animals; for example, horses, rabbits, giraffes, and more.

The following websites provide several puzzles for students to solve with their tangram pieces. These are just a few of the sites you and your students can find online.
http://www.tangram-channel.com/tangram-puzzles/
http://www.abcya.com/tangrams.htm
http://britton.disted.camosun.bc.ca/tangram.swf

Make a Tangram Handout

Use a sheet of tag board or cardboard to make your tangram.

1. Draw an 8" square on your paper.

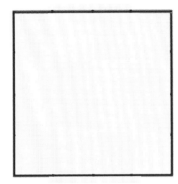

2. Divide the square into a lightly drawn 4 x 4 grid.

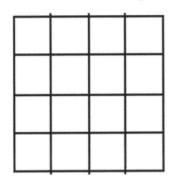

3. Draw the tangram pattern shown on the grid.

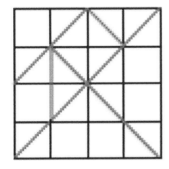

4. Cut the square into the seven pattern pieces.

Engineering Extension: Catapult Challenge

Student groups design and build a mini-marshmallow catapult. Catapults were once used in battle weapons to hurl rocks and other objects through the air to defeat enemies. Often they were placed on high ground and used to shoot rocks at castle walls. In this extension, students will first make a simple catapult to launch a cotton ball. After exploring different ways to build and use the catapult, student groups will design, build and test a mini-marshmallow catapult, re-engineering it as they try to make the best catapult they can.

Demonstrate how to build a very simple catapult that harnesses the potential force of the catapult by using kinetic energy to thrust a cotton ball into motion. Give each student a plastic spoon, a marker or a thick pencil, a craft stick, two rubber bands and a cotton ball. Follow these steps:

1. Crisscross a rubber band around the craft stick and the marker to attach them to one another.
2. Wrap the second rubber band around the spoon and attach to the end of the craft stick.
3. Put the cotton ball on the spoon and use the force of the bent spoon to release the cotton ball into the air.

Observe the speed and distance of the cotton ball, allowing a short amount of time for students to rearrange the materials to observe changes.

Divide the class into groups. Have the groups use their understanding of the operation of a catapult to create one that can launch a mini-marshmallow the greatest distance. Give each group the same set of materials: one plastic spoon, 25 rubber bands, 20 craft sticks and a few mini-marshmallows. There are many ways to build a catapult. Write the following project rules on the board or chart to build a free-standing catapult.

1. Test and revise the catapult by launching a mini-marshmallow at least 3 times to achieve the greatest distance.
2. You will have 30 minutes to get your catapult ready for competition.
3. You may use some or all of the provided materials.
4. You may tear or break any of the materials. No scissors allowed.

Assemble the class in an area with a long, straight smooth path. Each group shares its design before launching the mini-marshmallows. Students use a tape measure to record the distance from the launch area to the landing spot and record the results. Each team gets three chances. Students compute the average of their three attempts. When all marshmallows have been launched, analyze the results. Comparing results will lead to rich classroom discussions. Discuss the elements of the winning group's plan. What made it the most successful? Why? Explain why the mini-marshmallow in your group performed the way it did.

Try redoing the project another day with a different set of materials. Also try experimenting with heavier items, for example, a mini-marshmallow taped around a small paper clip. Here are two more material sets you may wish to try:

1. One paper cup, four craft sticks, 4 rubber bands, 2 paper clips, 12 inches of masking tape, one plastic spoon and some mini-marshmallows
2. Nine craft sticks, 6 rubber bands, one plastic spoon and some mini-marshmallows

Poetry Lesson for Math Awareness Month: Arithmetic

Arithmetic, the poem by Carl Sandburg, with its fresh and imaginative language, appeals to all children, young or old, with its fanciful and imaginary use of language. His descriptions call attention to arithmetic. It is a perfect poem for Math Awareness Month making the reader aware of arithmetic in a new light.

MATERIALS
- Carl Sandburg's Biography and excerpts and description of his poem *Arithmetic*
- Word processing or desktop publishing software or pencils, pens and paper

PLAN
- Read and discuss Carl Sandburg's biography and poem.
- Discuss the poem with the following questions:
    - How does Sandburg feel about arithmetic?
    - What arithmetic problems do you think he has the most trouble with? Explain your answer.
    - Where does Sandburg use humor in his poem?
    - What makes this poem enjoyable?

DO
Getting Ready to Write
Ask student what the world would be like without arithmetic. Write their responses on the board or a chart.

Writing the Poem
- Students write a poem in which they write about things in their everyday life that would change if arithmetic did not exist.
  For example: *I would not know how old I am, I could not count how many toes I have, I would not know how many planets there are in the sky, I would not be able to say how many teeth I am missing*
- Students title their poem "Without Arithmetic."
- Encourage line breaks so that the poem looks like a poem and not like a story.
- Continue their poem writing about all the things they would not know or could not do if arithmetic did not exist.

Editing and Publishing
- Students read and edit poems with partners.
- Students write their poem in a poetry book or enter them in a word processing program.
- Have students illustrate their final masterpiece.

Carl Sandburg Biography
January 6, 1878 – July 22, 1967

Sandburg is known as the poet of the Industrial Revolution. Carl Sandburg was born in Galesburg, Illinois. His parents, August and Clara Sandburg were immigrants from the north of Sweden. His parents were very poor and he had to leave school when he was thirteen to work. He took any job available. He worked in a theater, barbershop, in a brickyard, as a dishwasher in hotels and as a harvest hand in wheat fields. These jobs and the people he met through them became the subject matter of his poetry.

When Sandburg was 18 he visited Chicago and fell in love with it. Chicago and the Industrial Revolution were to become the subject of much of his poetry. Eventually he would win a Pulitzer Prize for his *Chicago Poems*, a collection of nine poems written about that city. He wrote about the beautiful skyscrapers and of the people who constructed and worked in them.

In 1897, when Carl was nineteen, he decided to see the country. Hopping on trains, he spent a year as a hobo. In 1898, when war with Spain was declared, Sandburg enlisted in the United States Army. After the war, he went to college and became interested in literature. Eventually, he became a journalist.

As a newspaperman, he struggled to keep writing poetry. Sandburg was unknown in the literary world until he was thirty-six years old. A group of his poems finally appeared in a famous poetry journal. A year later, his first book of poems was published. Those in the literary world thought he should pay more attention to the craft of writing. But the reading public appreciated his subjects and his honest words. In his lifetime, he won three Pulitzer prizes. Two of them were for his poetry and a third for a biography he wrote about Abraham Lincoln. In 1964, he received the Presidential Medal of Freedom from President Lyndon B. Johnson.

Arithmetic
by Carl Sandburg

In his poem *Arithmetic*, Carl Sandburg begins in a humorous way, letting the reader know his own difficulty with numbers as they "fly like pigeons in and out of your head." He can't get ahold of them. He also describes how sometimes you feel good "where the answer is right and everything is nice and you can look out of the window and see the blue sky." Other times you feel bad when "the answer is wrong and you have to start all over and try again and see how it comes out this time." This is a perfect poem for most children who have had wonderful moments with numbers and other times would have liked to forget that numbers exist. Students will enjoy reading the poem and enjoy Sandburg's humor as expressed in the last three lines of the poem:

> "If you ask your mother for one fried egg for breakfast and she
> gives you two fried eggs and you eat both of them, who is
> better in arithmetic, you or your mother?"

The entire poem is available online. You can search for it by typing the words *"Arithmetic* by Carl Sandburg*"* or you can go to the following website and find the poem. Print, copy and share with your class.

http://www.poemhunter.com/poem/arithmetic/

For a small fee, you purchase a movie of the poem *Arithmetic* from iTunes. In this movie, Carl Sandburg recites his poem as beautiful images appear that enhance his words. You can find the movie by entering the following URL:

https://itunes.apple.com/us/movie/sandburgs-arithmetic/id446316472

Additional Poems for Math Awareness Month

This traditional nursery rhyme *As I Was Going to St Ives* was published in the 18th century. St. Ives is thought to be in England, perhaps Cornwall or Cambridgeshire. The poem is a logic math riddle that over time became a children's nursery rhyme. Students read the poem and solve the math riddle. How many people are going to St. Ives? Assume that all people the man meets are going. How many living creatures other than people are going to St. Ives? How many possessions are going to St. Ives? How many people, creatures, and possessions are going to St. Ives? Your final answer is 2,802. Write your own poem replacing numbers, people, living creatures and possession with their own. Students solve each other's math riddles.

As I Was Going to St. Ives
by Anonymous

As I was going to St. Ives,
I met a man with seven wives,
Each wife had seven sacks,
Each sack had seven cats,
Each cat had seven kits:
Kits, cats, sacks, and wives,
How many were there going to St. Ives?

Mary Cornish in her poem *Numbers* introduces us to an original way of thinking about numbers. The entire poem is available online. Search for it or you can go to the following website and find the poem where it is ready to print, copy, and share with your class.

www.loc.gov/poetry/180/008.html

Numbers
by Mary Cornish

After reading the poem, have your students explore mathematical operations of addition, subtraction, multiplication and division. As Cornish does in her poem, select one or more mathematical operations and give that operation a personality. Write a stanza for that operation. Start with Mary Cornish's opening line: "I like the generosity of numbers."

APRIL LEARNING STANDARDS
Common Core Math

3.NBT.A.2 – Fluently add and subtract within 1000 using strategies and algorithms based on place value, properties of operations, and/or the relationship between addition and subtraction.	Reusing Old Textbooks – May the Forest Be With You
4.OA.A.3 – Solve multistep word problems posed with whole numbers and having whole-number answers using the four operations, including problems in which remainders must be interpreted.	Reusing Old Textbooks – May the Forest Be With You
5.NBT.A.3.B – Read and write decimals to thousandths.	Math in the Real World Scavenger Hunt
6.SP.B.5 – Summarize numerical data sets in relations to their context.	Math in the Real World Scavenger Hunt
6.EE.A.2.B – Identify parts of an expression using mathematical terms.	Math in the Real World Scavenger Hunt

Common Core Language Arts – Literature

RL3.1– Ask and answer questions to demonstrate understanding of a text, referring explicitly to the text as the basis for the answers.	*The Gladness of Nature* by William Cullen Bryant
RL.4.2 – Determine the meaning of words and phrases as they are used in a text including those that allude to significant characters found in mythology.	*Introduction to Songs of Innocence* by William Blake
RL.5.10 – Compare and contrast the experience of reading a story, drama or poem to listening to or viewing an audio or live version of the text including contrasting what they "see" and "hear" when reading the text to what they perceive when they listen or watch..	*The Gladness of Nature* by William Cullen Bryant
RL.6.6 – Describe how a narrator's or speaker's point of view influence how events are described.	*The Cloud* by Percy Bysshe Shelley
RL.7.5 – Analyze how a poem's form or structure contribute to it's meaning.	*Arithmetic* by Carl Sandburg

Common Core Language Arts – Writing

W.3.5 – With guidance and support from peers and adults develop and strengthen writing as needed by planning, revising and editing.	*The Cloud* by Percy Bysshe Shelley
W.4.2.D – Use precise language and domain specific vocabulary to inform about or explain the topics.	*The Gladness of Nature* by William Cullen Bryant
W.5.3.D – Use concrete words and phrases and sensory details to convey experiences and events precisely.	*The Gladness of Nature* by William Cullen Bryant

APRIL LEARNING STANDARDS
ISTE Technology Standards 2015

ISTE.1 – Creativity and innovation - Students demonstrate creative thinking, construct knowledge and develop innovative products and processes using technology.	Lesson – Going on a Camera Walk, Street Photography – Students work in photography groups to take digital photographs of interesting natural objects and outdoor activities they observe during the course of the day. They use the photos to create artistic slideshows.
ISTE.2 – Communication and collaboration – Students use digital media and environments to communicate and work collaboratively, including at a distance, to support individual learning and contribute to the learning of others.	Lesson – Earth Day Public Service Announcements (PSAs) – Student groups create an Earth Day public service announcement (PSA) using a variety of presentation software.
ISTE.3 – Research and information fluency – Students apply digital tools to gather, evaluate and use information.	Tantalizing Tangrams – Students create tables with word processing programs to show how many of the seven tangram pieces they use to make various shapes. They explore tangram sites on the Internet to find and solve tangram puzzles.
ISTE.4 – Critical thinking, problem solving and decision making – Students use critical thinking skills to plan and conduct research, manage projects, solve problems, and make informed decisions using appropriate digital tools and resources.	Lesson – Calorie Cavalcade – Students calculate calories in favorite foods using a variety of calorie counting websites. They create a chart using the information.

NGSS and ETS1 Science and Engineering Standards 2015

3-ESS2-1. – Represent data in tables and other graphical displays to describe typical weather conditions expected during a particular season	Catalog Poetry Weather and Climate – Students discover that weather is always changing and is reported everyday while climate is the average weather in a place occurring over a long period of time. They decide which data to use to plan what to wear tomorrow or plan a future vacation.
3-5-ETS1-1. – Define a simple design problem reflecting a need or a want that includes specified criteria for success and constraints on materials, time, or cost.	Drinking Straw Band – Student engineers design reed instruments from drinking straws and make music. They fine tune their instruments to create a melody to play for the class.
3-5-ETS1-2. – Generate and compare multiple possible solutions to a problem based on how well each is likely to meet the criteria and constraints of the problem.	Working in interest groups, research and design or improve a current invention using biomimicry.
3-5-ETS1-2. – Generate and compare multiple possible solutions to a problem based on how well each is likely to meet the criteria and constraints of the problem.	Catapult Challenge – Student groups design and build a mini-marshmallow catapult. Students first make a simple catapult. After exploring different ways to build and use the catapult, student groups will design, build and test a mini-marshmallow catapult, re-engineering it as they try to make the best catapult in the class.

May Monthly Holidays

American Bike Month • Asian/Pacific-American Heritage Month • Breath Easy Month • Flower Month • Foot Health Month • National Asparagus Month • National Barbeque Month • National Bike Month • National Egg Month • National Hamburger Month • National Mental Health Month • National Photo Month • National Physical Fitness & Sports Month • National Radio Month • National Salad Month • National Sight-Saving Month • National Strawberry Month • National Teaching and Joy Month Older Americans Month • Personal History Awareness Month • Project Safe Baby Month

May Weekly Holidays

First Week of May
Cartoon Art Appreciation Week • National Family Week • National Music Week • National Photo Week • National Postcard Week • National Volunteer Week • Pen-Friends Week International • Public Service Recognition

Second Week of May
Astronomy Week • Be Kind to Animals Week • Conserve Water/Detect-a-Leak Week • Deaf Awareness Week • Goodwill Industries Week • National Herb Week • National Historic Preservation Week • National Nurses Week • National Pet Week • National Postcard Week • National Teacher Appreciation Week • National Tourism Week • National Transportation Week • PTA Teacher Appreciation Week

Third Week of May
Art Week • Buckle Up America! Week • Girls Incorporated Week • National Bike Week • National Educational Bosses Week • National Historic Preservation Week • National Police Week • National Salvation Army Week • Public Relations Week • Public Transportation Week • Raisin Week • World Trade Week

Last Week of May
Anonymous Giving Week • Brotherhood/Sisterhood Week • International Pickle Week • National Backyard Games Week • National Frozen Yogurt Week • National Safe Boating Week • Pancake Week • Poetry Week

May Moveable Holidays

International Tuba Day.. first Friday

Mother's Day .... second Sunday

Hawaiian Song Day... second Sunday

National Teacher Day ....second Tuesday

Native American Day... second Saturday

Armed Forces Day .... third Saturday

International Jumping Frog Jubilee..................... third Saturday

Indianapolis 500 Auto Race.............Sunday before Memorial Day

Memorial Day..last Monday

Professional Secretaries Day ....Wednesday of the last full week

May Days for STEM Makers and Poets

	Day	Make and Do
1	Mother Goose Day	It's Mother Goose Day. Checkout the Mother Goose Society website and find out who Mother Goose was and how she changed over time. Mother Goose rhymes have more than likely passed down in folklore over time. Obtain Mother Goose rhyme books from the library. Using Maker Crafts, create a puppet theater and work with a group to perform the rhyme of your choice. Try your hand at creating your own Mother Goose rhyme in the style of Mother Goose.
2	Make-a-Book Day	Today is Make-a-Book Day. It is also the day that Benny Benson, a 7th grader entered a design for a flag for Alaska. His design won on this day in 1927. Would you like to become a vexillologist? A vexillologist studies the history of flags. Choose from various maker crafts to design a flag for your school or classroom. Your flag might be square, rectangular, or triangular. Research why it took 42 more years for the Alaska Territory to become a state and incorporate that into an illustrated book.
3	Famous Funnies Day	Makers of all ages love comic books and what a great day to create your own Famous Funnies, the first comic book published May 3, 1934. Web apps and software programs will get you started.
4	Movie Day	The Academy of Motion Picture Arts and Sciences was founded on this day in 1927. There are a world of maker activities for the budding maker photographer or videographer. There are many projects to build, from pinhole cameras to learning how to use your digital camera or other electronic devices to make movies. A good way to get started is to make a fifteen-second Public Service Announcement (PSA). Why not create a PSA to help curb bullying and/or cyberbullying at your school?

5	Cinco de Mayo	This Mexican national holiday celebrates a victory over the French at the Battle of Puebla, on May 5, 1862. A great day for do-it-yourself projects. Why not make a paper-mache piñata? You will need some newspaper strips, a balloon and a solution made out of boiled water and flour. Check online for recipes and directions.
6	National Teacher Day	The National Education Association (NEA) takes the lead on helping us recognize teachers across the United States. How will you celebrate the teachers who have made a difference in your life? Use social media to publicize activities at school or in your community. A great day for an essay contest for "A Teacher to Remember."
7	National School Nurse's Day	The National Association of School Nurses (NASN) is a great place to start to learn about the work that school nurses do to keep students healthy and safe everyday of the year. The NASN is on the forefront of issues important to all school-age youngsters. Why not interview your school nurse for a classroom newspaper?
8	World Red Cross Day	Learn about Henri Dunant and Clara Barton, great humanitarians. What is a humanitarian? Kids can make a difference through education, volunteering, writing letters and fund raising. What problems face your city? How can you solve them? How will you change the world?
9	Lost Sock Memorial Day	Today is the day to recognize your drawer of unmatched socks. Let's face it; they probably aren't coming back so why not make sock puppets today? Memorialize your missing socks, reflect upon how warm and fuzzy they made you feel and move on. Your sock puppets can put on a show in your very own do-it-yourself puppet theater. Every sock has a story to tell or a poem to recite.
10	Clean Up Your Room Day	This is the day that parents and teachers around the world wait anxiously for each year. Hopefully a few dust cloths and a little attention will get your classroom sparkling. You won't need shovels or industrial sized dumpsters. And when everything is nice and clean, write a little poem to parents to make sure they get their stuff cleaned up too. After all, Clean Up Your Room Day is a good day to practice what you preach.

11	Surrealistic Art Day	Salvador Domingo Felipe Jacinto Dali i Domenech, 1st Marques de Dali de Pubol was born on May 11, 1904 and died January 23, 1989). He is known as Salvador Dali and was a prominent Spanish Catalan surrealist painter born in Figueres, Spain. One of his most famous works, *The Persistence of Memory*, was painted in 1931 and has been part of the Museum of Modern Art (MoMA) in New York City since 1934. Study the painting and interpret what the painting means to you. Is it Einstein's *Theory of Relativity* or simply as Dali once responded, camembert cheese melting in the sun?
12	Limerick Day	Edward Lear's *Book of Nonsense* published in 1846 celebrates and popularizes limericks. Limerick is the third largest city in Ireland and limericks brighten our day especially on this day of Edward Limerick's birth. Limericks are humorous poems consisting of five lines. The first two lines rhyme with the fifth line. The third and fourth lines rhyme with each other. Poets, get out your pens! Here's a limerick from Edward Lear for inspiration: *There was an Old Man with a beard Who said, 'It is just as I feared! Two Owls and a Hen, Four Larks and a Wren, Have all built their nests in my beard!*
13	National Apple Pie Day	What is more American than apple pie? Pie is part of America's history and dating back to the earliest colonial settlers. Find out how apple pie became a national symbol. Also find a favorite recipe and learn how apple pie a la mode came to be. Does your family have a special apple pie recipe?
14	Stars and Stripes Forever Day	On this day in 1897 John Philip Sousa's famous march was played for the first time at Willow Grove Park outside of Philadelphia. Learn about Sousa, his life and his music. "Stars and Stripes Forever" is the official march of the United States of America. Find the original lyrics and the parody lyrics. "Be Kind To Your Web-Footed Friends" closed every episode of Sing Along With Mitch in the 1960s. Create your own Stars and Stripes parody.

15	United Nations International Day for Families	The United Nations proclaimed this day in 1993. The day provides an opportunity to raise awareness of family issues. Prepare a presentation on how families are important to the well-being of children and the challenges of overcoming issues of poverty and inequality.
16	Biographer's Day	Today marks the anniversary of the first meeting between Samuel Johnson and his biographer James Boswell. Johnson compiled the *Dictionary of the English Language*. His biography was published in 179. *The Life of Samuel Johnson* is considered to be the greatest biography ever written. Write a mini-biography of an inventor or a poet.
17	Pack Rat Day	Are you a pack rat? Make a list of all things that pack rats should do and not do today. For example, don't clean your room but do go to a garage sale.
18	International Museum Day	Organized by the International Council of Museums, over 35,000 museums in 143 countries participated in 2013. Museums engage their community with the ability to tell a story and engage their visitors. Design your own museum. Create a floor plan, poster and a brochure to describe your museum.
19	Malcolm X Day	In honor of the civil rights leader, who was born on this day in 1925. *The Autobiography of Malcom X* was published shortly after his assassination in February 1965. In 1998 *Time Magazine* named the autobiography one of the ten most influential nonfiction books of the 20th century.
20	Eliza Doolittle Day	Just you wait Henry Higgins! Eliza Doolitle is the Cockney Flower girl of George Bernard Shaw's *Pygmalion*, 1912, and Lerner and Lowe's *My Fair Lady*, 1956. After a chance meeting in Covent Garden, Eliza takes elocution lessons from Professor Higgins and most famously learns "The rain is Spain falls mainly in the plain." Search the Internet and find ten tongue twisters to help you improve your diction. Have a class elocution lesson led by student volunteers.

21	National Waiter and Waitresses Day	We recognize our restaurant servers today. Did you know that waiter's races have existed for over one hundred years? The races are part of French culture. With some plastic cups and trays, how about a cafeteria relay race today?
22	Sherlock Holmes	Arthur Ignatius Conan Doyle was born on May 22, 1859 in Edinburgh, Scotland. He created Sherlock Holmes, a London-based detective famous for his logical reasoning. Read some of his stories, apply your forensic science skills and create your own Sherlock Holmes mystery.
23	National Taffy Day	New Jersey resident Joseph Fralinger is credited with popularizing this confection made of molasses, vanilla and a variety of flavors. The candy is made by melting sugar, butter, water and cornstarch and pulling it into long strands. Research the legend behind why this treat is known as salt-water taffy and how it had its beginnings in Atlantic City.
24	National Escargot Day	Land snails cooked in butter and wine make for a tasty dish. The dish originated in Ancient Rome, but today the French consume 40,000 metric tons of snails a year. Let Escargot Day inspire you to write a story. How about How Snails Changed My Life?
25	National Tap Dance Day	On May 25 we celebrate tap dancing, a true American art form. Bill "Bojangles" Robinson, a significant contributor to tap dance, was born on this day. He is well known for dancing with Shirley Temple. He also starred in the 1943 movie Stormy Weather, loosely based on his life. Learn about the Orpheum Circuit, his Broadway and movie career and learn how to tap your troubles away. Can you Shim Sham Shimmy?
26	Birth Anniversary of Sally Ride	Sally Ride was born in Encino, California on this day in 1951. Sally was the first American woman in space. She earned a Ph.D. in physics in 1978 and was hired by the National Aeronautics and Space Administration (NASA). Would you like to travel into space?

27	San Francisco's Golden Gate Bridge	One of the most famous suspension bridges in the world, the Golden Gate Bridge opened on this day in 1937. Learn about the design and construction of this iconic bridge. Build a model bridge of your own. Which will you try: arch, cable-stayed, beam or suspension?
28	National Hamburger Day	Over 10 billion burgers a year are served in American restaurants each year and another 15 billion are consumed at home. Eating a burger on a bun probably started in Seymour, Wisconsin. Create your own burger. What would you put on your burger? Name your burger and create a marketing campaign to introduce it to the world.
29	Bing Crosby's White Christmas	Recorded on this day in 1942, Irving Berlin's song "White Christmas" recorded in just 18 minutes by Bing Crosby became the best-selling single of all time. With sales of over 50 million copies it's time to make a mash up. A "mash up" mixes several versions into a unique video. You Tube videos will get you started.
30	Lincoln Memorial Dedication Day	The Lincoln Memorial was dedicated on this day in 1922. Architect Henry Bacon modeled the memorial after a Greek temple known as the Parthenon. There are thirty-six exterior columns that symbolize the reunited states following the Civil War. There are three chambers that commemorate his presidency. Select an American president and design a Memorial.
31	American Poetry Day	Today celebrates the birthday of Walt Whitman in 1819 and honors all poets and poetry lovers. Walt Whitman was known for his free verse style of poetry. Hold a Poetry Day Pageant. Each class member selects a poem to memorize and perform.

May Holiday Lessons and Projects

May Day Lessons and Projects
Science Lesson: Constellations
Poetry Lesson: In May
by William Henry Davies
May Day is celebrated on May 1st as a traditional spring holiday in many cultures. In the merry month of May, April showers bring May flowers, baby birds spring to life and wildflowers paint the landscape. Students learn about May constellations and their myths. In the poetry lesson they write about a beautiful day in May.

Memorial Day Lessons and Projects
Technology Lesson: Thank You Letter
Poetry Lesson: From Liberty
by James Whitcomb Riley
We celebrate Memorial Day as a legal holiday in the United States. Memorial Day is a time for America to honor and remember those who have served our country. Students use word processing skills to write a letter to a veteran and write a poem describing a world where liberty exists.

Mother's Day Lessons and Projects
Engineering Lesson:
Poetry Lesson: Child and Mother
by Eugene Field
Mother's Day falls on the second Sunday in May. On this day we take time to honor our mothers and other mother figures in our lives. Students engineer pop-up cards and write a poem in which they take their mothers to a dreamland.

Wildflower Month Lessons and Projects
Math Lesson: Wildflower Calculations
Poetry Lesson: I Wandered Lonely as a Cloud
by Williams Wordsworth
National Wildflower Week celebrates nature's bounty of wildflowers. Students plant wildflowers and compare their growth and write poems describing wildflowers they see on an imaginary journey.

May – May Day Lessons and Projects

Science Lesson: May Constellations

Mankind has used the stars and the constellations that have formed for thousands of years, to help navigate across oceans, mark the changing seasons and know when to plant their crops. The first calendars were created using constellations as a guide. In this lesson, students learn about May's constellations, her "flock of stars" and their myths. Students work in pairs or in cooperative groups to research, plan and present a class constellation projects.

MATERIALS
- Reference books – constellations, astronomy
- Available technology – smartphones, computers, tablets, iPod touches, etc.
- Desktop publishing and/or multimedia software and available presentation software – PowerPoint, HyperStudio, KidPix 3D, Acrobat, etc., or online programs like Prezi.
- White board and/or chart paper, markers, black construction paper
- Small gold stars or glow-in-the-dark sticker stars
- White chalk, crayons and/or colored pencils

PLAN
- Review the brainstorming process with your class.
- As a class, have students share their previous knowledge about stars and constellations.
- Students describe any experiences they may have had observing constellations.
- Discuss formats that their cooperative group reports might take. Elicit responses from your students. You may wish to begin with a few ideas for students to adopt and adapt. For example:
    - a constellation report as if the constellation were for sale
    - a television advertisement incorporating advertising techniques
    - an oral report with visuals
    - a written report
    - a group diorama
    - a travel poster
    - a brochure offering sight-seeing adventures to your constellation.

Classroom Chart

Prepare a classroom chart listing the seven May constellations.

The Seven Constellations of May

Canes Venatici – The Hunting Dog
Centaurs – The Centaur
Coma Berenices – The Hair
Corvus –The Crow
Crux – The Southern Cross
Musca –The Fly
Virgo – The Maiden

Group Project Chart

As a class, prepare a chart of the various elements for each group project:

May Constellation Project

Your group's constellation
The members of your group
Illustrations of your selected constellation
Description of where it is located in the May sky
Description of what the constellation's name means
Description of the constellation's appearance
Description of any legend connected to your constellation

DO

- Divide the class into cooperative groups of five students. For smaller classes, divide student into triads. Try to have enough groups so that all seven May Constellations will be studied and presented.
- Each group will create a report on a selected or assigned constellation. The group will select the format of the report.
- Students create the group report using available presentation software.
- Students present their reports.

EXTENDING THE LESSON

- Students create their own original constellations using black construction paper, gold or white glow-in-the-dark stars, and/or other craft or drawing materials.
- Students create a short myth telling the story of their constellation. Create as a written report, podcast or video.
- Post to a class web page or print to DVD.

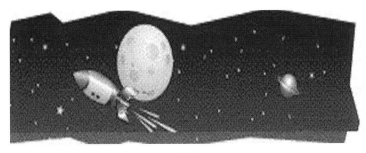

May Day STEM Extensions

Technology Extension: Mother Goose Day

In the merry month of May
　　When green leaves begin to spring,
Little lambs do skip like fairies,
　　Birds do couple, build, and sing.
In the Merry Month of May
　　　-　Traditional Nursery Rhyme

Each year, National Mother Goose Day is celebrated on May 1st. Founded in 1987 by Gloria T. Delamar and listed on several holiday calendars, Mother Goose Day is celebrated across the United States. Its purpose is "to re-appreciate the old nursery rhymes." And this is its motto: "Either alone or in sharing, read childhood nursery favorites and feel the warmth of Mother Goose's embrace." In this extension, students find out about the origins of Mother Goose and choose from a variety of Mother Goose activities.

Who was Mother Goose?
No one is sure whether Mother Goose was a real person. What can you learn about Mother Goose? What key words will you use? Word process a paragraph about what you learned along with citations of the websites you used.

Mother Goose – Illustrated
There are many beautifully illustrated Mother Goose books. Check your local library for books illustrated by Randolph Caldecott, Raymond Briggs, Helen Oxenbury, Alice and Martin Provensen, just to name a few. Compare how different illustrators depict the same character. Create your own Mother Goose illustration in your favorite drawing program. Try Storybird.com.

Mother Goose Goes Digital
Collections of nursery rhymes began to appear in the 18th century. Write your own mixed-up rhymes. Update one of your favorite rhymes to make it relevant to today's culture. For example, what would happen if your favorite nursery rhyme characters had the technology you have? Rewrite a rhyme of your choice. For example:
　　　　　Mary had a smart phone,
　　　　　The coolest in the town,
　　　　　And everywhere that Mary went
　　　　　She never put it down.

A New Classic
Add lines to some classic rhymes. Many nursery rhymes leave characters in perilous situations. For example, what happens to Humpty Dumpty when all the King's horses and all the King's men couldn't put him back together again? What about the wife of Peter Peter Pumpkin Eater? Does she live forever inside the pumpkin shell? Try adding lines to some classic Mother Goose Rhymes. Create a new and improved rhyme.

Find the Themes
Find examples of Mother Goose rhymes for each of the following themes:
a.	Animals	b.	Bedtime	c.	Food
d.	Holidays and Seasons	e.	Places to Go	f.	Riddle Rhymes
g.	Things Around Us	h.	Weather		

Engineering Extension: Maypole Constructions

May Day celebrations evoke memories of Maypoles. Maypoles were once common all over England where they were erected to last from one year to the next. Many maypoles still exist in England where maypole dances welcome in the month of May year after year. School children practice for many weeks, dancing around the maypole, weaving the ribbons strung from the top of the pole. You can view maypole dances on YouTube and dance steps on the web.

In this engineering extension, students are presented with a maypole project design problem. They have been asked to present a proposal for a maypole design. Working in groups, students assume the work of construction engineers. The groups survey the grounds for an ideal spot to place the maypole and build scale models using materials that represent those of their finished maypole design. They will make sketches, diagrams and plot plans as they build their models and prepare their proposals. Groups present the completed proposals to the class. The class acts as a Maypole Celebration Committee and gives feedback about the presented designs and models.

Display the following proposal requirements on a board or chart.
1. The maypole must be able to be placed on an available site on the school grounds.
2. The models must be built to ¼ scale for a twelve-foot pole.
3. Use a wrapping paper roll cut to the scaled size of three feet.
4. Decorate the pole using wrapping paper, tissue paper, crepe paper and stickers.
5. Use clay or small boxes to secure the base of the maypole.
6. Staple or glue an even number of thin ribbons to the top of the pole; cut the ribbons to twice the length of the pole.
7. Create a pole top decoration using any combination of available materials such as paper, felt and flowers.
8. Prepare presentations that include a site plan, the maypole model and a paragraph that describes the site proposed, the actual materials that will be used and any special features.

Have each group give a presentation of their scale maypole model. Place the finished models along with the descriptive paragraphs in the classroom.

Math Extension: Hawaiian Lei Day

While people around the world celebrate May Day on the first day of May, Hawaiians are celebrating Lei Day. The tradition began in 1927 when two newspaper columnists Don Blanding and Grace Tower Warren suggested the holiday. It was Grace that coined the term "May Day is Lei Day." Each Hawaiian Island produces a unique lei made of flowers generic to their island. Kauai's lei is made of purple berries. Maui's lei is made from the fragile pink Hawaiian rose. The Big Island of Hawaii's flower is red ohia and is the most traditional of all. Oahu's lei is made of the yellow ilima flower, often called the "Royal Lei" as it was worn by Hawaiian royalty.

In this extension students work in groups and use math skills to design and produce leis in celebration of Lei Day. To produce the leis, students use geometry tools to create circles, measurement skills to determine straw lengths, fraction knowledge to fold flowers and design patterns to make unique leis. Divide the class into small groups. Have the groups select the tissue paper color they will use to make the lei flowers. Distribute the following materials to each group:
1. Tissue paper (in the color or colors they selected)
2. Math compass (one per student)
3. Four inch squares of tag board or heavy card paper (one per student)
4. Sharpened pencil (one per student)
5. Embroidery needle (one per student)
6. Ruler (one per student)
7. Scissors and tape
8. Three or four drinking straws
9. Embroidery floss thread
10. Pony beads

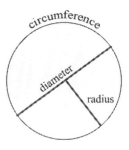

Students learn to use a math compass to draw a circle. Draw a circle on the board and define the terms circumference, diameter and radius. During a teacher-led demonstration, students use the compass to draw a three-inch circle on the cardboard. Here are the steps to follow:
1. Tighten the hinge on the top of the compass to prevent slippage.
2. Insert the pencil into the holder.
3. Make the tip of the pencil even with the sharp point of the compass.
4. Tighten the screw on the pencil holder to firmly secure the pencil point.
5. Place the pencil point and the compass point to a spread of 1½ inches on the ruler. This will be the radius of your 3" circle.
6. Find the center point of the square.
7. Hold the compass firmly at the hinge and place the pointed end of the compass on the center point to draw a 3" circle.
8. Slowly and carefully rotate the compass to draw the circle.

Have group members follow the directions on the Hawaiian Lei Day Handout to create leis. Group members wear the finished leis. Play Hawaiian music and have the class dance in a Lei Day parade.

Hawaiian Lei Day Handout

Work together as a group to delegate tasks below to complete the project. As a team, create the most efficient way to work.

1. Cut out the tag board circles to use as your pattern.

2. Put tissue paper into three sheet stacks, one on top of another.

3. Place the patterns on top of the tissue paper stacks and trace around them.

4. Cut out the tissue paper stacks. Each stack will make one flower. You will need as many flowers as it will take to complete the length of your lei (approximately 30 to 40 flowers).

5. Fold the circles in half and then in half again as many times as possible to create pleats before unfolding.

6. Measure and cut the straws into ¼ inch segments. The numbers of straw segments need to be equal to the number of three-ply tissue circles.

7. Measure the length of embroidery floss you will need for each lei by laying a segment in a circle around the tallest group member's neck. Add an additional three inches.

8. Cut the thread to the measured length for each group member.

9. Complete the flowers as follows:

    a. Separate three strands from the embroidery floss.

    b. Thread the strands into the embroidery needle.

    c. Place a piece of tape on the other end of the floss to prevent the items you sew from falling off.

    d. Alternate stringing pony beads, straw segments and tissue flowers to create the lei.

    e. Carefully push the needle straight through the middle of the flower as you proceed.

    f. Knot the ends to finish the lei.

Poetry Lesson for May Day:
In May

William Henry Davies suggests that May is the time to "spend the livelong day with nature."
In his poem *In May*, William Henry Davies imagines himself sitting under a tree on a typical
day and celebrating nature by sharing bread with birds, listening to their songs and watching
cows in the meadow. Davies escapes the everyday crowded world to a cottage near an ocean
and listens to birds that sing rather than to the voices of men. In this poetry lesson, students
write a poem about a beautiful day in May.

MATERIALS
- William Henry Davies Biography and his poem *In May*
- Word processing or desktop publishing software (optional)

PLAN
- Read and discuss the biography and poem.
- How does William Henry Davies use imagery to draw a picture of this day with words?
- Which words convey that this is the month of May?
- What mood does the author evoke and which phrases tell this to the reader?

DO
Getting Ready to Write
- Students draw a detailed picture of a beautiful day in May that includes placing
  themselves into the picture. Their picture will be used as the inspiration for their own
  poem.

Writing the Poem
- Encourage students to make their poems as descriptive as their drawings by using
  interesting adjectives, active verbs and modifying adverbs.
- Have students include where they are in their picture, what they will do and see.
- Share in pairs or in a small group how it feels to be a part of their drawing.

Editing and Publishing
- Students edit their writing by checking adjectives, verbs and adverbs to make sure they
  are as descriptive as possible.
- Students publish their poems and share them with the class.
- Create a month of May anthology to print or for use on a class web page.

William Henry Davies Biography
July 3, 1871 – September 26, 1940

William Henry Davies was born in Newport, Monmouthshire, Wales. He had an older brother and a younger sister. His father died when he was three years old and his mother remarried. William's mother felt that the care of three children was too difficult for her so William and his two siblings were reared by his grandparents. He was not an obedient child. When William was twelve years old, he along with five of his school friends were caught stealing a purse. He was arrested.

His grandmother wanted him to be a frame maker but this type of work bored him. He didn't want the dreary life that so many of the poor people he grew up with endured. He dreamed for something more. William longed to go to America and he worked hard to save enough money to go.

William travelled from England to America and eventually to Canada, much of the time as a hobo. He travelled back and forth across the Atlantic Ocean on cattle boats at least seven times. He probably would have never stopped traveling except an accident derailed his plans. He lost his foot jumping from a train in Canada He sailed back to England and supported himself as a street singer.

Most of Davies' poetry is about his adventures as a hobo. He never married and spent most of his time alone. His writing included wonderful descriptions of nature. He also wrote about life's hardships and the characters that he met on his travels. He wrote directly and innocently, even in a childlike way. His work reflected his love of life.

William Henry Davies self-published his first book of poetry and his reputation as a great poet began. Davies was well-liked in the literary world and made many friends. Although Davies never graduated from college, at the age of 55 he received an honorary degree from the University of Wales. Davies accomplished what he set out to do and he lived an extraordinary life.

In May
by William Henry Davies

Yes, I will spend the livelong day
With Nature in this month of May;
And sit beneath the trees, and share
My bread with birds whose homes are there;
While cows lie down to eat, and sheep
Stand to their necks in grass so deep;
While birds do sing with all their might,
As though they felt the earth in flight.
This is the hour I dreamed of, when
I sat surrounded by poor men;
And thought of how the Arab sat
Alone at evening, gazing at
The stars that bubbled in clear skies;

And of young dreamers, when their eyes
Enjoyed methought a precious boon
In the adventures of the Moon
Whose light, behind the Clouds' dark bars,
Searched for her stolen flocks of stars.
When I, hemmed in by wrecks of men,
Thought of some lonely cottage then
Full of sweet books; and miles of sea,
With passing ships, in front of me;
And having, on the other hand,
A flowery, green, bird-singing land.

Additional May Day Poems

Robert Burns wrote poems and songs. In his poem, *The Charming Month of May*, the character Chloe is a heroine of a Greek novel written in the second century. She is a sweet and charming orphaned girl. Burns describes her eyes as outrivaling the May sun.

Students work together to identify all of the descriptive words in the poem. For example, you will find *charming, fresh, youthful, peaceful, and feather'd*. Use as many of the words as you can to write a descriptive paragraph about the month of May.

The Charming Month of May
By Robert Burns

It was the charming month of May,
When all the flow'rs were fresh and gay
One morning, by the break of day
The youthful, charming Chloe-
From peaceful slumber she arose,
Girt on her mantle and her hose,
And o'er the flow'ry mead she goes-
The youthful, charming Chloe.

Chorus – Lovely was she by the dawn,
Youthful Chloe, charming Chloe,
Tripping o'er the pearly lawn,
The youthful, charming one.

The feather'd people you might see
Perch'd all around on every tree,
In notes of sweetest melody
They hail the charming Chloe;
Till, painting gay the eastern skies,
The glorious sun began to rise,
Outrival'd by the radiant eyes
Of youthful, charming Chloe.
Lovely was she, &c.

Traditionally, each month is associated with a gemstone. The month of May is the emerald, a symbol of rebirth. Why is the green emerald a good choice for May? The following three stanzas are part of the minstrel ballad, *Robin Hood and the Monk,* and this section is often titled *May in the Green-Wood.* The original poem was written in Middle English, a variety of English spoken from 1066 until the late 15th century and appears first below. Try writing your own poem using some of the Middle English words. You will also see a modern day translation.

May in the Green-Wood
Anonymous, 15th Century

In somer when the shawes be sheyne,
    And leves be large and long,
Hit is full merry in feyre forste
    To here the foulys song.

To se he dere draw to the dale
    And leve the hiles hee,
And shadow him in the leves grene
    Under the green-wode tree.

Hit befell on Whitsontide
    Erly in a May mornyng,
The Sonne up faire can shyne,
    And the briddis mery can syng.

May in the Green-Wood
Modern Translation by Lenny Koff

In summer when groves are beautiful
    and leaves are large and long [full],
it is delightful to hear the birds sing
    in the fair forest;

To see the deer come to the dale
    and leave the high hills,
shadowing themselves among green leaves
    under the greenwood tree.

It happened on Whitsuntide
    early on the May morning;
the fair sun was shining
    and merry birds were singing.

May – Memorial Day Lessons and Projects

Technology Lesson: Writing a Thank You Letter To a Service Member or Veteran

Students learn about Memorial Day in this letter-writing lesson. To honor men and women who have served or are currently serving in the military, students write and illustrate thank you letters. Organizations exist to distribute these letters. In this lesson students will work in groups to select one of the organizations. Each student will write a letter following the guidelines of the organization selected.

MATERIALS
- Computer with Internet connection
- Word processing software
- Drawing materials – colored pencils, crayons, markers, and so on.
- Handout – Writing to Active Service Members and Veterans

PLAN
- Begin a class discussion by asking the class to share reasons they are thankful for the contributions of active troops and veterans.
- Discuss the importance of showing support, appreciation and respect for our military on Memorial Day.
- Tell students they will be working in groups to select an organization from the list on the Writing to Active Service Members and Veterans Handout.
- Distribute and discuss the handout.

DO
In a group, select the organization and individually compose a letter in word processing software. Students begin their letter as follows:
- DATE – Start with the date.
- INSIDE ADDRESS – Use a school address and teacher's name.
- SALUTATION – The letters are given randomly so use a generic salutation such as "Dear Service Member," "Dear Hero," or "Dear Brave One."
- BODY – Begin the letter by thanking the veteran and/or active service member. Include some of the following information:
  - School – grade, favorite subjects, activities
  - Favorite things – movies, sports, music, and so on
  - Family – brothers, sisters, parents, grandparents
  - Life in their town or city
- CLOSING – For example, Sincerely yours, Yours truly, and so on.
- SIGNATURE – Students print, sign and add student artwork.

Writing to Active Service Members and Veterans Handout

One of the easiest ways to send letters of thanks, gratitude and well wishes is to send them through one of the organizations dedicated to this work. Have your group visit the following sites and review their letter writing criteria and suggestions. Select the organization of your group's choice. Each member of the group writes an individual letter that is reviewed by your group and your teacher for format and content before sending.

Operation Gratitude
https://www.operationgratitude.com/writeletters/
Operation Gratitude has sent over 150,000 care packages filled with snacks, entertainment, hygiene and hand-made items, plus personal letters of appreciation. The letters are sent to new recruits, veterans, first responders, wounded Warriors, and care givers to U.S. Service Members deployed overseas. The website gives further information. Be sure to click on the "Letter Writing Flyer."

A Million Thanks
http://www.amillionthanks.org/send_a_letter.php
A Million Thanks has sent over seven million thank you letters to troops around the world. Their mission is to keep sending letters as long as necessary. Go to the website, review the content, sample letters, dos and don'ts and the "Who We Are."

Flags Across the Nation
http://www.flagsacrossthenation.org/our-projects/letters-to-the-troops/
Flags Across the Nation asks parents, teachers, children and patriots to write letters to deployed troops and recovering soldiers. On their site is a flag stationary template that students can download and use for their letters.

Memorial Day STEM Extensions

Science Extension for Memorial Day:
D-Day, the Moon and the Tides

In this extension lesson, students will read and discuss how the moon and the tides influenced the decision to select November 6, 1944 as D-Day. They will learn about the phases of the moon and discuss the reason why the invasion took place during the spring tide of the full moon. Students complete a foldable flap Phases of the Moon Worksheet in which they draw and describe the phases of the moon.

The D-Day invasion of Normandy during World War II has been said to be the most carefully planned military operation in world history. The battle was designed to free France from Nazi control. To do this, the troops of countries allied against Germany needed to launch a combined aerial and amphibious assault across the English Channel. In choosing the invasion date of November 6, 1942, General Dwight D. Eisenhower relied on the expertise of a team of astronomers and meteorologists. They had specific criteria for the phase of the moon, the tides and the time of day to begin the invasion. They determined that they needed a full moon for illumination. A time shortly before dawn was selected because the tides would be changing from low tide to high tide. This would insure that any German booby traps would be visible. November fifth was selected as a date that met the criteria, however, the weather and visibility were not ideal and the mission was pushed forward to November sixth. Although there were many casualties during the invasion, D-Day was a successful beginning to the end of the German occupation of Europe.

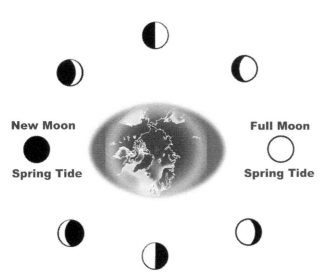

New Moon

Spring Tide

Full Moon

Spring Tide

Because the sun shines on the moon as it does on the earth, at any given time half the moon is in darkness and half is in light. As the moon rotates around the earth, we see only part of its daylight half. Every evening a different part of the moon's daylight half becomes visible to us and we see a slightly different phase of the moon. The moon's rotation around the earth along with the sun and the phases of the moon are the major factors in the creation of tides. When the sun, moon and earth all line up at the new or full moon the result is the "spring" tide which are the highest tides and lowest tides. When the moon is at first or third quarter the effect on the tides is less, causing lower high tides and higher low tides. These are known as "neap" tides. Since the planners of the D-Day invasion wanted the tides, moon, and time of day to be ideal, they had to select a full moon spring tide. The full moon gave the allies the perfect illumination, as it is the only moon phase that sets at sunrise.

Phases of the Moon Worksheet

Write a description of the moon's phases named on the inside rectangles. Include information about the corresponding tides. Cut on all bold solid lines. Fold flaps on dotted lines to the centerline. Draw the phases you described on the top fold of each flap.

	Waxing Gibbous	Full Moon	
	1st Quarter	Waning Gibbous	
	Waxing Crescent	3rd Quarter	
	New Moon	Waning Crescent	

Engineering Extension: Squishy Circuits

Wireless radio came of age during WWI as a source of news and entertainment. Military leaders recognized the importance of this communication with infantry and ships at sea. Initially the radio could not transmit speech and only used Morse code to send messages back and forth between ships and land stations. During the war years the radio became more powerful and compact. After the war, radio use continued to grow. Even though today's radios use sophisticated electronics to operate, the basic principles of electricity used in the first wireless radios, are at their core.

In this lesson, student engineers will work in four groups and become circuit designers. They will use two different kinds of homemade play dough to demonstrate electrical properties by lighting up LEDs and spinning motors. To get ready, play the AnnMarie Thomas four-minute TED Talk video to your students. Dr. Thomas is the creator of squishy circuits. View the video at http://www.ted.com/talks/annmarie_thomas_squishy_circuits. This talk is also available at http://squishycircuitsstore.com/kits.html. On the TED site you are able to download the video to your computer. The video is in English; however, you can easily download the video with subtitles in a variety of languages. English language learners benefit from seeing the video with English subtitles to improve reading skills. In the video, Dr. Thomas shows how homemade play dough can be used to demonstrate the principles of electricity. The video will provide your students with an excellent overview of what you are about to do.

Below are the supplies you will need to create squishy circuits for demonstration and group work. The electronic components can be purchased online at sites such as www.adafruit.com, squishycircuitsstore.com and Amazon.

1.   Five, nine-volt battery with lead wires for each group or five AA battery packs
2.   An assortment of LEDs (light emitting diodes), 10mm
3.   Five hobby motors
4.   Cooking source such as hot plate
5.   Medium size pot and two large bowls
6.   Measuring cups
7.   Measuring and mixing spoons
8.   5 lbs. flour
9.   2 lbs. sugar
10. 26 oz. container of salt
11. Gallon of distilled water
12. 1 ½ oz. cream of tartar
13. 16 oz. vegetable oil
14. Gallon size plastic zip bags or air-tight containers

Preparation of the Conductive Dough and the Insulating Dough

Students assist the teacher in preparing two different dough recipes. The recipe with salt and cream of tartar conducts electricity whereas the recipe with sugar blocks the flow of electricity. Using the dough, students design circuits that will turn motors and light LEDs. Students volunteer to assist with the measuring, mixing, pouring, stirring and kneading the conductive and insulating doughs.

Dough Recipes

Conductive Dough (uses salt and cream of tartar)
Ingredients needed to make approximately six balls of dough.
- 4 cups tap water
- 6 cups flour
- 1 cup salt
- 12 tablespoons Cream of Tartar
- 6 tablespoons vegetable oil
- Food coloring

Directions
1. Mix four cups of flour and all ingredients except the food coloring in a pot and cook over medium heat on a hot plate.
2. Stir vigorously and scrape the bottom and sides constantly to avoid burning.
3. Keep stirring until the mixture forms into a ball in the center of the pot.
4. Let it cool slightly.
5. Knead the remaining two cups of flour into the ball until the desired consistency is achieved.
6. Stir in a small amount of food coloring.
7. The ball can be stored in an airtight container or plastic bag until ready to use.

Insulating Dough (uses sugar)
Ingredients needed to make approximately six balls of dough.
- 2 cups distilled water
- 6 cups flour
- 2 cups sugar
- 12 tablespoons vegetable oil
- Food coloring (a different color than conductive dough)

Directions
1. Mix four cups of flour and all ingredients except the food coloring in a bowl.
2. Mix in two tablespoons of distilled water and stir.
3. Keep adding distilled water into the mixture until the dough absorbs a majority of the distilled water.
4. Knead the mixture into one lump and add remaining water, continuing until it has a sticky-like texture.
5. Add the remaining two cups of flour and knead the dough until a desired texture is obtained.
6. Stir in a small amount of food coloring using color other than the color of the conductive dough.
7. The ball can be stored in an airtight container or plastic bag until ready to use.

Teacher Demonstration and Student Explorations

Divide each dough into six smaller balls in order to have one set to use in demonstration and five sets to distribute to five groups. Begin with a classroom demonstration. For the demonstration:

1. Show and describe each squishy circuit component that the students will be using.
   a. Conductive dough – Used to conduct the flow of electricity.
   b. Insulating dough – This dough is not conductive. Electricity must go around this dough to complete a circuit.
   c. Battery Pack – The power source for the circuits.
   d. Motor – The motor converts the electric energy into motion.
   e. LEDs (Light Emitting Diodes) – Components that will light up.
2. Student volunteers demonstrate lighting LEDs with conductive dough.
   a. Take a lump of conductive dough and insert the red and black wires from the battery pack into opposite sides of the dough while placing a LED into the dough. It will light up.
   b. Take the LED and the wires out of the conductive dough and divide the dough into two separated lumps. Note that the LEDs have two terminals, one longer than the other. Attach each terminal to a different lump.
   c. Now attach one wire into each lump. Make sure that the longer LED terminal is paired with the red wire from the battery pack. If it is, the LED will light up.
   d. Next, take the two pieces of dough and push them together. Note that when you push the two pieces of dough together, the LED light goes out because a short circuit has been created.
3. Divide the class into five groups. Distribute the insulating dough and the remaining conductive dough, LEDs, batteries and motors to each group. Have student groups make and experiment with squishy circuits by following the directions below:
   a. Take a piece of insulating dough and two pieces of conductive dough. Make a sandwich where the insulating dough is in the middle.
   b. Place the battery wires into the top and bottom of the dough sandwich.
   c. Insert the LEDs into the "bread" of the sandwich remembering that the red wire should be nearest to the longest LED terminal. If it doesn't work, keep tinkering until it does.
4. Group Exploration:
   a. Give each group time to explore using the materials to build more squishy circuits. A fun project is to design an animal whose eyes light up and tail wags.
   b. For additional project ideas, have groups use available technology to visit the Squishy Circuit website at http://courseweb.stthomas.edu/apthomas/SquishyCircuits/

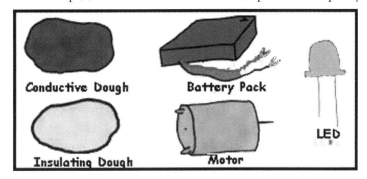

Math Extension: Savings Bonds

In 1935, President Franklin D. Roosevelt signed legislation creating the first "baby bond" program. United States Savings Bonds encourage participation by Americans in government financing and to promote savings. The E series of defense bonds were sold to contribute to the financing of World War II. On December 7th, 1942, the Japanese attacked Pearl Harbor. The bonds were renamed war bonds. American citizens were stimulated by advertisements and celebrity endorsements to purchase the bonds. School children saved quarters on a cardboard card with 75 slots ($18.75). When the card was full, they went to the post office and received a $25 war bond that matured in ten years, a 2.9% return on their investment. Billions of dollars worth of war bonds were sold. Savings bonds are still a good method for a small investor to save without a lot of risk. Today, bonds are sold online at Treasury Direct, http://www.treasurydirect.gov/indiv/products/prod_eebonds_glance.htm. Here you will find out information about Series EE savings bonds.

In this extension, students will create a savings plan using a spreadsheet or a calculator. War bonds were sold for $18.75. Savers had cards where they could insert a quarter for 75 days.

It takes 75 quarters ($18.75) to purchase a savings bond that will be worth $25.00 after ten years. Using this fact, create a spreadsheet that will help you see how much you will have saved if you saved 25 cents a day for a year. Determine how many savings bonds you could purchase at the end of the year. How many could you purchase if you saved 50 cents a day? Seventy-five cents a day? A dollar-a-day? How much was your investment and how much was your return on your investment?

What if you did the same thing each year for ten years. What would you have at the end of twenty years?

Poetry Lesson for Memorial Day: Liberty

In his poem *Liberty* James Whitcomb Riley introduces us to the beauty of a land where Liberty lives. Riley personifies "Liberty" and describes its power. He asks the birds to celebrate freedom by singing of the gifts experienced in a free land. Riley also commands the Independence Bell to ring telling "Of love and Liberty!" Students write a poem describing a world where liberty exists.

MATERIALS
- James Whitcomb Riley Biography and Excerpt from his poem *Liberty*

PLAN
- Read and discuss James Whitcomb Riley's biography and poem.
- Brainstorm with students and discuss the following:
- What does the world look like where "Liberty" lives? Ask students what objects in nature would they want to command? As they brainstorm, encourage students to use interesting adjectives, verbs and adverbs in their descriptions to make their poems interesting and original.

DO
Writing the Poem
- Have students write poems of their own using "Where Liberty Lives" as the title.
- Students write their poems describing their beautiful, joyful and magical world. Remind them to use interesting parts of speech.

Editing and Publishing
- Have students read and edit poems with partners.
- Students will create a class poetry book of their poems along with an illustration. Have each student create a page for the book by orienting a piece of paper sideways. Students divide the paper in half, write their poems on the left side of the page and illustrate on the right side. Place all of the poems into a class book. If you decide to do each student page on a computer, use the landscape selection in the page set-up.

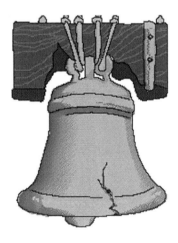

James Whitcomb Riley Biography
October 7, 1849 – July 22, 1916

James Whitcomb Riley was born in a log cabin in Greenfield, a small village in Indiana. His father was a lawyer and politician. He probably developed his love and talent of writing poetry from his mother. His parents worried about him because he was not a good student. He seemed incapable of learning mathematics or history. When he was young, one of his teachers asked him where Christopher Columbus sailed on his second journey. He answered that he didn't even know where Columbus sailed on his first journey.

Riley's father wanted him to be a lawyer but he could not keep his mind on law books. Instead he became a poet writing verses for signs as he traveled the American Middle West. He became the wealthiest writer of his time and one of the most well known as his poems were illustrated beautifully in books. Riley loved to be on stage and perform his writing. People who heard him were enthralled by the magic of his performance and didn't want to leave his presence.

During his childhood, he was surrounded by "American folks." He loved to listen to these "folks" tell their happy, sad and imaginative tales. He was called a "dialect singer," using their expressions in his poetry. He was also called "The Hoosier Poet" (a poet from Indiana) and also "The Children's Poet." He never lost the child in him and children could identify with the whimsy that lived in his poetry. When Riley was growing up, Annie, an ophan, lived with him and his family. In the evenings, she would tell stories about "wunks" who lived in the ground and goblins and fairies who lived under the stairs. Riley wrote *Little Orphant Annie*, one of his most famous poems, influenced by Annie's stories. *Little Orphaned Annie* would be the inspiration for *Little Orphan Annie*, the comic strip, a radio program, television programs, plays and movies.

Riley died in 1916 of a stroke. President Woodrow Wilson wrote a note to Riley's family conveying the sadness of much of the people in our country: "With his departure a notable figure passes out of the nation's life; a man who imparted joyful pleasure and a thoughtful view of many things that other men would have missed."

Excerpt from the Poem Liberty
by James Whitcomb Riley

. . .
'Sing! every bird, to-day!
Sing for the sky so clear,
And the gracious breath of the atmosphere
Shall waft our cares away.
Sing! sing! for the sunshine free;
Sing through the land from sea to sea;
Lift each voice in the highest key
And sing for Liberty!'

'Ring! Independence Bell!
Ring on till worlds to be
Shall listen to the tale you tell
Of love and Liberty!

. . .
O Liberty, it is thy power
To gladden us in every hour
Of gloom, and lead us by thy hand
As little children through a land
Of bud and blossom; while the days
Are filled with sunshine, and thy praise
Is warbled in the roundelays
Of joyous birds, and in the song
Of waters, murmuring along
The paths of peace, whose flowery fringe
Has roses finding deeper tinge
Of crimson, looking on themselves
Reflected - leaning from the shelves
Of cliff and crag and mossy mound
Of emerald splendor shadow-drowned.
We hail thy presence, as you come
With bugle blast and rolling drum,
And booming guns and shouts of glee
Commingled in a symphony
That thrills the worlds that throng to see
The glory of thy pageantry. . .

Additional Poems for Memorial Day
The Gettysburg Address

In his Gettysburg Address, Abraham Lincoln memorializes soldiers who made sacrifices for freedom that we enjoy today. It was delivered on November 19, 1863 in Gettysburg, Pennsylvania to dedicate the site of the Soldiers' National Cemetery there. After reading, students discuss why the Gettysburg Address is still relevant today.

The Gettysburg Address
A speech by Abraham Lincoln

Four score and seven years ago our fathers brought forth on this continent, a new nation, conceived in Liberty, and dedicated to the proposition that all men are created equal.

Now we are engaged in a great civil war, testing whether that nation, or any nation so conceived and dedicated, can long endure. We are met on a great battle-field of that war. We have come to dedicate a portion of that field, as a final resting place for those who here gave their lives that that nation might live. It is altogether fitting and proper that we should do this.

But, in a larger sense, we can not dedicate – we can not consecrate – we can not hallow – this ground. The brave men, living and dead, who struggled here, have consecrated it, far above our poor power to add or detract. The world will little note, nor long remember what we say here, but it can never forget what they did here. It is for us the living, rather, to be dedicated here to the unfinished work which they who fought here have thus far so nobly advanced. It is rather for us to be here dedicated to the great task remaining before us – that from these honored dead we take increased devotion to that cause for which they gave the last full measure of devotion – that we here highly resolve that these dead shall not have died in vain – that this nation, under God, shall have a new birth of freedom – and that government of the people, by the people, for the people, shall not perish from the earth.

The poem *Memorial Day 1892,* written by Fredrick W. Emerson, commemorates the sacrifices soldiers make in defending our country. After reading the poem, students honor soldiers by building a Wall of Remembrance. Each student creates a brick out of a third of a piece of red construction paper. On their brick, each student writes a paragraph about why it is important to remember our veterans. The bricks can be stapled on a bulletin board to form a wall.

Memorial Day, 1892
by Frederick W. Emerson

Our nation is reverently thinking to-day
Of the loved ones sleeping beneath the cold clay;
Of the sacrifice made, and the brave deeds done,
To preserve our Union as a glorious one.
We ne'ever will be able to pay the great cost
Of the noble, the true, and the brave that we've lost;
But over their graves, with tears like the dew,
We'll lay our sweet flowers of red, white and blue.

Our Nation is paying its tribute today
Upon the green mounds where its loyal men lay;
While statesmen, and orator, fondly repeat
The story of those who knew no defeat.
They tell of the Union united again,
By the triumph of those who died not in vain;
Of the forty-four states, all loyal and free,
Of the peace, and the freedom, from sea to sea.

Our Nation is thinking, rejoicing, to-day,
While comrades are kneeling their tribute to pay;
And heart once sorrowing, rejoice now to see
The "Star Spangled Banner," the flag of the free.
For out of their loyalty and brave deeds done,
Out of their battles and their victories won,
Came freedom and peace, and in liberty's name
Our banner floats freely, with glory and fame.

Our Nation is reverently thinking to-day
Of the men now living who'll soon pass away;
Like the grass of the field and the flowers they spread
O'er the graves of their comrades, immortal, dead.
Tall monuments stand to their memory dear,
But they crumble and fall, like the leaf when sere;
Our Nation united forever will stand,
To those who preserved it, a monument grand.

Wherever we gather to-day 'neath "The Stars,"
Let's honor the living now wearing the scars
Which they brought from the fields of battle and strife,
While protecting "Our Flag," and our Nation's life.
Let the flowers bear tribute in their simple way,
And each one remember Memorial Day;
Remember the dead, and the living, though few,
Who fouht 'neath "The Stars," and the red, white and blue.

May – Mother's Day Lessons and Projects

Engineering Lesson: Pop-Up Cards

In this engineering lesson for Mother's Day, students learn the mechanics of creating simple pop-up cards. After sharing their first designs, students explore more complicated patterns and examples on the web. Their subsequent designs will be more intricate with further tinkering. Students construct their card and write a Mother's Day greeting on the inside of the card. They will create fancy envelope liners. The finished card will be ready to gift to their mothers or a special mother figure in their life.

MATERIALS
- Scissors, rulers
- Pencils, Markers
- Construction paper, 8 ½" x 11"
- Greeting card envelopes, #9, 5 ¾" x 8 ¾"
- Tagboard, 12" x 18"
- Students bring giftwrap paper in advance, minimum size, 12" x 18"

PLAN
Distribute scissors, markers and construction paper to each student. Have students create a simple pop-up card as you demonstrate the following:
1. Fold the construction paper in half.
2. Beginning at the centerfold, cut two sets of parallel lines of equal height on each side. Good heights for the cuts are about one third up toward the top of the card.
3. Open the card and pull the two flaps into an upright position.
4. Rub fingers along the edges of the flaps to deepen the creases at all the folds.
5. Use color construction paper and the markers to create decorations for each flap.
7. Cut out decorations and paste on the inside flap.
8. Have students share and discuss their pop-up cards.

DO
Search for Ideas
Divide the class into pairs to search the Internet for other instructions and ideas to make more intricate cards. The following site has instructions for making many types of pop-up cards: http://wp.robertsabuda.com/make-your-own-pop-ups/. Students can also view some inspiring pop-up designs at www.lovepopcards.com.

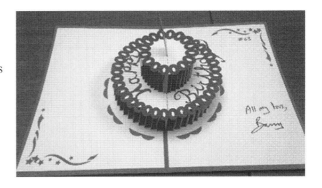

Make a Card

1. Each student makes a card. Their finished card must fold and pop-up.
2. Write a message on the inside of the card. Refold the card and decorate the front by repeating some of the decorations used for the pop-up design.
3. Write "Happy Mother's Day" on the front of the card.
4. Decorate the back of the card. Decorating the back gives the card an extra oomph and provides space for students to promote themselves as the card maker.

Creating Decorative Envelopes with Liners

Making the Envelope

After students have shared the finished cards with classmates, they do the following to create fancy giftwrap envelopes:

1. Distribute a #9 greeting card envelope (5 ¾" x 8 ¾") to each student.
2. Students carefully disassemble the envelopes and open all the way.
3. Trace the envelope with a pencil onto a sheet of tagboard to create a sturdy envelope template. Cut out the template.
4. Students flip the giftwrap paper making it back side up.
5. Trace the envelope template onto the backside of the wrapping paper with a pencil and cut along the pencil guidelines.
6. Reassemble the envelope. Students fold in the two side flaps. Using a glue stick they apply glue to the outer edge of the bottom flap and the two side flaps. Turn up the bottom flap to cover the side flaps. Crease all folds tightly by rubbing their fingers over the folds.

Making the Liner

Add an envelope liner. Students do the following to create the liner:

1. Trace the envelope template they made onto a new piece of tag board.
2. Trim the new template by cutting ¾ inch off the bottom and 1/8 inch from each side. This allows the liners to easily slide into the envelopes.
3. Trace the trimmed template (liner template) onto the back side of a new sheet of wrapping paper.
4. Cut out the wrapping paper liner and insert it into the envelope.
5. Fold down the flap to check for size and do any additional trimming as necessary.
6. Verify the size and use a glue stick to place glue around the backside of the liner to make it secure.

Finishing the Gift

1. When the glue is completely dry, insert the pop up cards into the envelopes.
2. Fold and seal the top flap.
3. The Mother's Day cards are ready to gift.

Mother's Day STEM Extensions

Science Extension: Honeycomb Candy

In this extension lesson, students learn about chemical reactions while making delicious Honeycomb Candy as a Mother's Day gift. Students observe the preparation of the candy. When the mixture is very hot, sodium bicarbonate or baking soda is added to produce carbon dioxide. Students observe bubbles forming in the mixture and the mix almost doubling in size. This is due to the carbon dioxide escaping from the solution. The bubbles are trapped in the mixture and the result is a crisp candy with a honeycomb appearance. Students giftwrap the candy in cellophane and create a Mother's Day label for their delicious gift.

Honeycomb Candy Ingredients
1. ¾ cups sugar
2. 2 tablespoons water
3. 2 tablespoons honey
4. 1½ teaspoons baking soda or sodium bicarbonate

Supplies
1. Baking tray with sided edges
2. Large saucepan
3. Candy thermometer
4. Hot plate
5. Protective gloves for the teacher

Directions
Students observe the teacher doing the following.
1. Line a baking tray with foil.
2. Place a large saucepan on a hot plate set on low.
3. Spread the sugar across the bottom of the large saucepan.
4. Sprinkle the water and honey over the sugar. Stir until the sugar dissolves.
5. Increase the heat when the sugar dissolves and continue to cook without stirring. Be very careful as the mixture becomes extremely hot.
6. The bubbles get larger as the heat increases and the mixture changes to an amber color.
7. Remove the mixture from the heat at 300°F.
8. Quickly whisk the baking or bicarbonate of soda into the hot syrup.
9. Watch how the mixture foams up with bubbles as it reacts to the addition of the baking soda.
10. Quickly pour the syrup into the baking tray with sided edges and allow to cool.

Students complete the following steps.
11. Break the honeycomb into small pieces.
12. Divide the pieces and place on paper napkins to distribute to each child.
13. Students taste a piece and wrap the rest in clear cellophane paper.
14. Have students create a label for their candy gift.

Technology Extension: Mary Cassatt Paintings

Impressionist painter Mary Cassatt was a famous American artist who lived much of her adult life in France where she befriended the Impressionist artists and studied and exhibited with them. She is well-known for her wonderful drawings and paintings of mothers with children. Students will work in groups to create a slide show of Mary Cassatt paintings. After viewing the slideshows, they will paint a watercolor using her art as a model.

In this extension, students will need:
1. Computer with Internet capability and presentation software
2. Watercolors
3. Water
4. Brushes
5. Small paper plates
6. Pencils
7. Art paper
8. Photographs of students and important adults (requested before beginning the lesson)

Students follow these steps to make a slideshow:
1. Working in groups, students search the Internet to find images of Mary Cassatt's paintings of mothers and children.
2. Select eight paintings and import them into a slide show.
3. Add music, text and transitions.
4. Present their slide show to their classmates.

Discuss Cassatt's technique of drawing her subjects with pencil sketches and finishing with watercolors. Follow these steps to create a painting in the style of Mary Cassatt as a gift for Mother's Day.
1. Distribute watercolors, water and brushes to students.
2. Students create a background watercolor wash before beginning their pencil sketch.
3. When the background wash is dry, they are ready to sketch their portrait in pencil.
4. Students who have brought photographs place the photos by their paper and sketch them with pencils. Those without photographs will sketch from memory. Students imagine themselves in a special moment with their important person as they sketch.
5. Paint their sketches with watercolors.
6. Mix colors on the paper plate to achieve just the right shade.
7. Remind students to clean their brushes between colors before going to a new area.
8. The finished pictures are mounted on colored art paper and gifted on Mother's Day.

Created with smilebox.com

Math Extension: Flower Power – Flower Bar Graph for Mother's Day

This flower bar graph will make a wonderful Mother's Day gift. You will need a piece of one-inch graph paper per student, colored construction paper, scissors, glue, markers or crayons, and tape measures or measuring sticks.

Have students do the following:

1. In the classroom, students measure each other and record their measured height.
2. At home, measure and record the height of each member of the family.
3. Begin your bar graph by leaving a two-inch border at the bottom of your graph paper.
4. Construct your graph so that you begin numbering with 0 feet at the bottom and continue up the left in ½ inch increments up to 8 feet.
5. Each ½ inch equals ½ foot and this can be placed in the bar graph key.
6. Write the name of each family member under the graph, evenly spaced. Don't worry about staying within the grid lines.
7. Draw a line to represent the height of each person on the graph. The lines become the stem of a sunflower.
8. The middle of the sunflower is where you will place a drawing of each family member.
9. Finish the graph by adding the graph key, leaves, petals and pictures for the background.
10. Mount the graph on a 9" x 12" piece of construction paper.

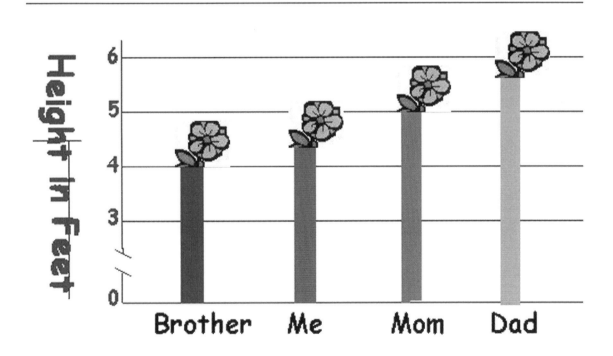

179

Poetry Lesson for Mother's Day: Child and Mother

The poem *Child and Mother* by Eugene Field is a perfect poem for Mother's Day. On Mother's Day we take time to celebrate our mothers or a prominent mother figure. In this poem, the child describes a perfect place where he would like to take his mother. He refers to it as a Dreamland where all her responsibilities dissolve and where all sorts of magical things occur to soothe her. Your students write a poem inviting their mothers or a person they love to this perfect place where their everyday problems disappear. They present their finished poem as a Mother's Day gift.

MATERIALS
- Eugene Field Biography and poem *Child and Mother*
- Word processing or desktop publishing software (optional) and printer

PLAN
- Read and discuss Eugene Field's biography and poem.
- Discuss the poem using the following possible questions:
  - What makes this land a "Dreamland?"
  - What does this beautiful land look like?
  - The boy says that the "Dreamland" is "out yonder." Where is "out yonder?"
  - Why does the boy repeat "out yonder" at the end of the poem?

DO
Getting Ready to Write
Have students respond to the following sample questions:
  - Where is your dreamland?
  - What about your land makes it seem dreamlike?
  - What chores that exist in your mother's real life would disappear in your dreamland?
  - How will you make this land magical?

Writing the Poem
- Students write poems of their own suggesting they refer to the brainstorming list on the board or the chart.
- Using Eugene Field's poem as a model, suggest students begin their poems with the first line replacing the words "out yonder" with the location of their dreamland.
- Students continue their poems describing their dreamland.
- Suggest that they include what they would do for their mothers in this land both real and magical.

Editing and Publishing
- Have students read and edit poems with partners.
- Make a class Mother's Day Anthology with student poetry and present it to parents. Include each poet's name, the title of their poem and an illustration.
- As a class, students think of a name for their anthology.

Eugene Field Biography
September 2, 1850 – November 4, 1895

 Eugene Field was born in St. Louis, Missouri. His father was an attorney who was famous for his defense of a slave who sued for his freedom. This case is sometimes referred to as "the lawsuit that started the Civil War." His mother died when Eugene was only two years old and his cousin in Massachusetts raised him and his brother. His father died when Field was 19. At that time, he was attending college but dropped out. He enrolled in and dropped out of two other colleges. He unsuccessfully tried his hand at acting. Eugene also studied law for a while but gave that up as well.

With an inheritance his father left him, he traveled to Europe and returned having used up all of the money. Shortly after his return, he worked as a journalist for the St. Joseph Gazette in Missouri. That same year he married Julia Comstock with whom he had eight children. He eventually became city editor of the Gazette and then went to work for many newspapers. He served as an editorial writer at the Morning Journal and then at the Times Journal. For a short amount of time he was the managing editor of the Kansas City Times and then for two years worked as editor of the Denver Tribune. Field eventually moved to Chicago and wrote a humorous newspaper column for the Chicago Daily News. He became famous for his humorous language.

Field was also well known for his childhood poetry published in famous magazines. After his first poem *Christmas Treasures* was published, more than a dozen books of poetry followed. He became known as the "poet laureate" of children and the "poet of childhood."

Many memorials honor him including a park, elementary schools and statues depicting his poems among which are his two most famous *The Duel* and *Wynken, Blynken, and Nod*. Many of his poems were set to music and became commercial successes. Some of his works were inspirations for paintings by Maxfield Parrish, a famous artist of the 20th century.

Child and Mother
by Eugene Field

The Dreamland that's waiting out yonder.
We'll walk in a sweet posie-garden out there,
Where moonlight and starlight are streaming,
And the flowers and the birds are filling the air
With the fragrance and music of dreaming.

There'll be no little tired-out boy to undress,
No questions or cares to perplex you,
There'll be no little bruises or bumps to caress,
Nor patching of stockings to vex you;
For I'll rock you away on a silver-dew stream
And sing you asleep when you're weary,
And no one shall know of our beautiful dream
But you and your own little dearie.

And when I am tired I'll nestle my head
In the bosom that's soothed me so often,
And the wide-awake stars shall sing, in my stead,
A song which our dreaming shall soften.
So, Mother-my-Love, let me take your dear hand,
And away through the starlight we'll wander, --
Away through the mist to the beautiful land,--
The Dreamland that's waiting out yonder.

Additional Mother's Day Poems

In his poem, *God's Masterpiece Is Mother*, Herbert Farnham describes his mother as a masterpiece created by God. He describes the patience, strength and beauty that is his mother as "the gentleness of morning dew," "the majesty of a tree," and "the calm of a quiet sea." Students create an impressionistic portrait of their mother surrounded by nature. They use one of the lines of the poem as their inspiration and write the line on the painting. For example, if their mother reminds them of the "quiet of the sea" they may choose to draw a sea with their mother's eyes in the quiet waves. Or if they see their mothers as "the majesty of tree," they may wish to draw tree trunks as their mothers.

God's Masterpiece Is Mother
by Herbert Farnham

God took the fragrance of a flower...
The majesty of a tree...
The gentleness of morning dew...
The calm of a quiet sea...
The beauty of the twilight hour...
The soul of a starry night...
The laughter of a rippling brook...
The grace of a bird in flight...
Then God fashioned from these things
A creation like no other,
And when his masterpiece was through
He called it simply - Mother.

In his poem, *Mother o' Mine*, Rudyard Kipling describes his mother's unconditional love. Do you have unconditional love towards any living thing? Look at Kipling's examples and think of three examples of your own.

Mother o' Mine
by Rudyard Kipling

If I were hanged on the highest hill,
Mother o' mine, O mother o' mine!
I know whose love would follow me still,
Mother o' mine, O mother o' mine!

If I were drowned in the deepest sea,
Mother o' mine, O mother o' mine!
I know whose tears would come down to me,
Mother o' mine, O mother o' mine!

If I were damned of body and soul,
I know whose prayers would make me whole,
Mother o' mine, O mother o' mine!

May – Wildflower Month Lessons and Projects

Math Lesson: Wildflower Calculations

This unit integrates planting and growing wildflowers with the study of fractions. Students categorize the growth of the wildflowers in categories (colors, sizes, types) and express the results in fractional terms. During this unit, students should be able to apply their knowledge of fractions to the real world.

MATERIALS

- Large aluminum baking pans, one for each group
- Potting soil, wildflower seeds, water
- Paper cups, index cards, markers, rulers
- Counting Flowers Worksheet One and Worksheet Two

PLAN

- Divide class into groups of five.
- Distribute aluminum baking pans, wildflower seeds in paper cups, potting soil index cards, markers and rulers.

DO

- The groups will do the following:
  - Write the names of the group members on an index card and affix to the pan.
  - Spread ¼ inch of soil on the bottom of the aluminum pan and sprinkle the seeds over the soil.
  - Cover the seeds with a thin layer of soil. One quarter inch of soil works well.
  - Gently water the soil to keep moist without overwatering.
- Keep the aluminum pans in a warm, lighted place.
- When the plants are grown, groups complete the Counting Flowers Worksheet One.
- After completing Worksheet One groups complete Worksheet Two.

Counting Flowers Worksheet One

Names: _____

You will need rulers and colored pencils or crayons. Draw a picture of your flowers in the box below.

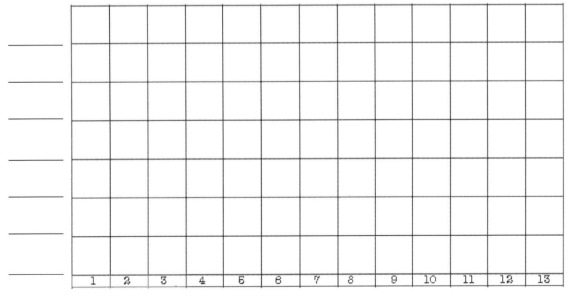

Count the colors of your wildflowers. Create a bar graph below to illustrate the results.

Colors

	1	2	3	4	5	6	7	8	9	10	11	12	13

Counting Flowers Worksheet Two

Write fractions to represent your results. For example, there are 14 flowers altogether. If 2 flowers are red, 2/14 of the flowers are red. Reduce to the lowest common denominator. Write the color of flowers along with the appropriate fraction in the box below.

Measure the tallest flower and the shortest flower.
Write the measurements in inches. _____ _____
Find the difference between them. _____

Write three word problems relating to the flowers with your group. Include both the questions and the answers.

_____

_____

_____

_____

_____

_____

_____

Wildflower Month STEM Extensions

Science Extension:
Drying and Preserving Wildflowers

In this lesson students will gain an understanding of the natural process by which wildflowers are mummified and fossilized. Wildflowers are plants that grow in their natural state without interference from man. Those growing in the wild are not planted or tended in gardens. Because many types of wildflowers weather quickly, the ideal method for collecting is to go on a class nature walk. Encourage students to pick only what they need so that the wildflower bed will remain intact. Have them include leaves in their collections. Students create bookmarks using the dried wildflowers.

The oldest and still considered to be one of the best drying agents is sand that is almost salt free. The problem with sand is that it is heavy and can cause bruise the drying flowers. To prevent bruising students will use a mixture containing equal parts of borax and cornmeal and will add two tablespoons of salt to their mixture. Divide students into four groups. Provide materials and directions for each group.

Materials
Cornmeal, two five-pound boxes
Borax, two 65-ounce boxes
Salt
Measuring cups, measuring spoons and mixing bowls, paintbrush, foil pans, one per group
Wildflowers

Directions for Drying Wildflowers
1. Pick wildflowers with some leaves and thin stems.
2. Look for plants that have as little water on them as possible.
3. Mix four cups of Borax and four cups of cornmeal.
4. Add two tablespoons of salt.
5. Spread a one-inch layer of the mixture evenly over the bottom of the foil container.
6. Gently arrange the flowers and the leaves in separate spots on top of the mixture.
7. Carefully sprinkle the remaining mixture over the flowers so that they are covered.
8. Seal the pan with plastic wrap or tin foil and tape in place.
9. Place in a cool spot and wait about 2 weeks.
10. Gently remove the flowers.
11. Use the paintbrush to carefully remove any remaining mixture from the flowers.

Making a Wildflower Bookmark
Cut two rectangles from a sheet of self-adhesive plastic slightly larger than the traditional 2" x 6" bookmark size. Peel the backing off one piece and lay it sticky side up on a flat surface. Carefully place the pressed flowers on the sticky side of the plastic. Peel the backing off the second side and gently place the sticky side on top of the dried flowers. Draw a 2" x 6" rectangle at the edge of the plastic. Using a scissors, trim the final bookmark.

Technology Extension: Scratch Flowers

Using Scratch, students learn mathematical and computational ideas as they create animations, games, music, art and interactive stories. Students practice the design process as they execute their Scratch projects. They imagine, create, experiment, share, reflect and reimagine. Students start with an idea and build a working prototype. They experiment and debug to tweak their projects to the desired results.

The best way to learn Scratch is to work with it. Go to http://scratch.mit.edu and click on "How To Make A Project." Do the interactive tutorial and you will gain what you need to get started with Scratch. You can see examples and you may also join the Scratch online community for free. Once you have a username and password, you can post your projects and see other projects. You can easily view the blocks that make up a project. This will help you learn even more.

Challenge your students to create flowers using Scratch. Log-in to the scratch site. Students will quickly learn by looking at some example flower projects when they type "flowers" in the Scratch search engine. They will create building blocks that they can repeat in their designs. Once they have successfully created a script to build a flower, have them create a field of wildflowers.

Additional resources can be found at the ScratchEd Community at http://scratched.gse.harvard.edu. At this site, watch the short Get Started with Scratch video to see more of the amazing things you can do with Scratch.

Engineering Extension:
Product Engineers

Working as product engineers, student groups will design and manufacture perfumes made from wildflowers. They will perform a preliminary fragrance test of many wildflowers and select one to produce in quantity. After recording a recipe for the chosen perfume, students will decide on a name for the fragrance. They will "manufacture" a number of sample vials with labels for classmates to try.

Many wildflowers are quite fragrant. Each group will gather and test the perfume quality of the collected flowers as follows:

1. Gather as many fragrant wildflowers as possible to test. Some of the most common and flavorful are African daisy, California poppy, Marigold, rose petals, sagebrush leaves, lavender. Try to collect samples of at least three wildflowers from the local area.
2. Chop one type of wildflower at a time using a food chopper and a cutting board.
3. Fill a baby food sized jar with lid to the top with the chopped flower and add a combination of water and alcohol until the jar is full. Screw on the lid.
4. Repeat the steps above with one or two other kinds of wildflowers.
5. Wait two or three days and strain the liquid using a cheesecloth or a coffee filter
6. Try the perfumes. Select the one with the best fragrance to refine.
7. Replace the lid and allow the fragrance to sit for another day or two. Give it a final test. If it needs to have more strength, add more chopped flowers and repeat step 3 through 5 with the strengthened product.
8. Write a recipe for the final product including how many flowers and how much water and alcohol is needed.
9. Choose a name for the perfume that describes its essence.

Supply the groups with several 1ml. perfume sample vials. They are available in sets of 100 on the Internet. Amazon.com is a good source. Each groups follows its recipes to create four or five samples for their classmates to test. The recipes are distributed. Students can use the recipes to create wildflower recipes for themselves or their family members or maybe to make a gift for Mother's Day.

Poetry Lesson for Wildflower Month:
I Wandered Lonely as a Cloud

William Wordsworth loved nature and all its delights. In his poem, *I Wandered Lonely as a Cloud*, Wordsworth captures the glory of the golden daffodils. Students will wander in his world and visualize the wonders that the viewing of daffodils growing wild brought to him. They will then take an imaginary journey of their own and write a poem describing wildflowers they come upon.

MATERIALS
- William Wordsworth Biography and his poem *I Wandered Lonely as a Cloud*
- Word processing or desktop publishing software or pencils, pens and paper

PLAN
- Read and discuss William Wordsworth biography and poem.
- Discuss the poem with the following questions:
  - Why does Wordsworth compare the way he is walking to a cloud?
  - How do the daffodils make him feel?
  - Where does he use personification?
  - How does Wordsworth feel when he is old and sees the daffodils again? Why?

DO
Getting Ready to Write
- Have students close their eyes and imagine themselves in a beautiful place such as a garden, a tropical forest, a park. Have them begin to look at the landscape until they arrive at some extraordinary wildflowers.
- They can continue viewing whatever else is in this beautiful place, paying attention also to what they hear.
- Discuss what the students saw and heard when their eyes were shut. Write their examples on the board.
  For example: *wildflowers purple, red and blue, the golden sun, owls hooting, ocean roaring.*
- How would they add personification to what they saw? Write examples on the board.
  For example: *dancing wildflowers purple red and yellow, the sun waving goodbye to the clouds*

Writing the Poem
Using *I Wandered Lonely As A Cloud* as a model, students write poems of their own.
Encourage line breaks so that the poem looks like a poem and not like a story.
- Begin poems by using the words I wandered or I floated or a similar phrase.
- Continue their poem describing what the wildflower looks like and what they are doing.
- Continue describing other things they saw or heard along the way.
- Use personification to make their descriptions interesting and vivid.

Editing and Publishing
- Students read and edit the poems with partners.
- Make crepe paper wildflower and attach to bulletin board or tag board and place edited poems on the board. For instructions on how to make crepe paper wildflowers go to this website: http://appetitepaper.com/paper-wildflowers-yellow-day-dreaming/

William Wordsworth Biography
April 7, 1770 – April 23, 1850

William Wordsworth was born in Cumberland in North West England, a rural paradise. This environment influenced Wordsworth's love of nature and became the subject of much of his poetry. His father was a wealthy landowner. As a child, he had two traumatic experiences. He lost his mother when he was eight and lost his father when he was thirteen. He had five siblings.

Wordsworth published his first poem when he was seventeen at the same time as he completed his studies at Cambridge. He then went to France where the French revolutionary ideas intrigued him. Because of tensions that were mounting between England and France, Wordsworth moved back to England. Eventually he married Mary Hutchinson and had five children with her.

He remained very close to his siblings especially Dorothy. William wrote the poem *I Wandered Lonely as a Cloud* after walking with her among the daffodils. This experience was also recorded by Dorothy in her journal.

Wordsworth was a major English Romantic poet and helped to launch the Romantic period in English literature. His poetry reflects the Romantic poets view of nature's healing properties. He was a poet concerned with the human relationship to nature. He became England's Poet Laureate in 1843 and remained so until his death.

Wordsworth believed that nature strengthens our character and allows us to see the mysteries of the universe. He also believed that nature once experienced remains in our memory forever. These memories can give people as much joy as when they were first experienced. He wrote that the world of things was "forever speaking." We have to listen and look to find a "tale in everything."

I Wandered Lonely As A Cloud
by William Wordsworth

I wandered lonely as a cloud
That floats on high o'er vales and hills
When all at once I saw a crowd,
A host, of golden daffodils;
Beside the lake, beneath the trees
Fluttering and dancing in the breeze.

Continuous as the stars that shine
And twinkle in the milky way,
They stretched in never-ending line
Along the margin of the bay:
Ten thousand saw I at a glance,
Tossing their heads in sprightly dance.

The waves beside them danced; but they
Out-did the sparkling waves in glee:
A poet could not but be gay,
In such a jocund company:
I gazed --- and gazed---but little thought
What wealth the show to me had brought:

For oft, when on my couch I lie
In vacant or in pensive mood,
They flash upon that inward eye
Which is the bliss of solitude;
And then my heart with pleasure fills,
And dances with the daffodil

Additional Poems for Wildflower Month

In his poem *Song of the Flower*, Khalil Gibran writes a description of a flower in the first person. At the end of the poem he writes about its wisdom: "But I look up high to see only the light, /And never look down to see my shadow/This is wisdom which man must learn." Students write a paragraph explaining what wisdom people can learn from flowers.

Song of the Flower
by Khalil Gibran

I am a kind word uttered and repeated
By the voice of Nature;
I am a star fallen from the
Blue tent upon the green carpet.
I am the daughter of the elements
With whom Winter conceived;
To whom Spring gave birth; I was
Reared in the lap of Summer and I
Slept in the bed of Autumn.

At dawn I unite with the breeze
To announce the coming of light;
At eventide I join the birds
In bidding the light farewell.

The plains are decorated with
My beautiful colors, and the air
Is scented with my fragrance.

As I embrace Slumber the eyes of
Night watch over me, and as I
Awaken I stare at the sun, which is
The only eye of the day.

I drink dew for wine, and hearken to
The voices of the birds, and dance
To the rhythmic swaying of the grass.

I am the lover's gift; I am the wedding wreath;
I am the memory of a moment of happiness;
I am the last gift of the living to the dead;
I am a part of joy and a part of sorrow.

But I look up high to see only the light,
And never look down to see my shadow.
This is wisdom which man must learn.

In the poem *Wayside Flowers*, William Allingham writes about the unexpected gifts that flowers bring to the passersby. He asks people to leave these flowers in the places where they are found so that travelers will profit from them. In this lesson, students will write about an incident that they remember when they picked a flower that didn't belong to them and knew they shouldn't. How did they feel and what was the situation?

Wayside Flowers
by William Allingham

Pluck not the wayside flower,
It is the traveller's dower;
A thousand passers-by
Its beauties may espy,
May win a touch of blessing
From Nature's mild caressing.
The sad of heart perceives
A violet under leaves
Like sonic fresh-budding hope;
The primrose on the slope
A spot of sunshine dwells,
And cheerful message tells
Of kind renewing power;
The nodding bluebell's dye
Is drawn from happy sky.
Then spare the wayside flower!
It is the traveller's dower.

Alfred Lord Tennyson was the most popular poet of the Victorian era during the reign of Queen Victoria, 1832- 1901. He was beloved by the queen and was knighted. Tennyson knew that in all creation there are similarities and if we could unfold the mystery of the creation of a flower, we could unfold the mysteries of the creation of the human species. How are flowers and humans alike? How are they different? Draw a Venn diagram to illustrate your responses. What does the diagram tell you?

Flower in the Crannied Wall
by Alfred Lord Tennyson

Flower in the crannied wall
I pluck you out of the crannies
I hold you here, root and all, in my hand,
Little flower — but if I could understand
What you are, root and all, and all in all,
I should know what God and man is.

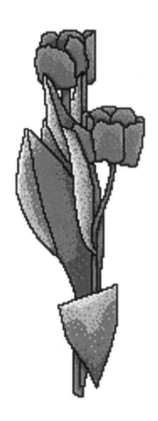

MAY LEARNING STANDARDS
Common Core Math

4.OA.A3 - Solve multistep word problems posed with whole numbers and having whole-number answers using the four operations, including problems in which remainders must be interpreted	Wildflower Calculations
4.MD.A.2 - Use the four operations to solve word problems involving distances, intervals of time, liquid volumes, masses of objects, and money, including problems involving simple fractions or decimals, and problems that require expressing measurements given in a larger unit in terms of a smaller unit.	Savings Bonds
5.G.B.3 - Understand that attributes belonging to a category of two-dimensional figures also belong to all subcategories of that category.	Lei Day: Geometry
5.MD.B.2 - Make a line plot to display a data set of measurements in fractions of a unit (1/2, 1/4). Use operations on fractions for this grade to solve problems involving information presented in line plots.	Flower Power Bar Graph for Mother's Day
6.RP.A.3.C - Find a percent of a quantity as a rate per 100 (e.g., 30% of a quantity means 30/100 times the quantity); solve problems involving finding the whole, given a part and the percent.	Savings Bonds

Common Core Language Arts – Literature

RL.3.1 – Ask and answer questions to demonstrate understanding of a text, referring explicitly to the text as the basis for the answers	*Liberty* by James Whitcomb Riley
4.2 – Determine a theme of a story, drama, or poem from details in the text; summarize the text.	*Child and Mother* by Eugene Field
R.L.5.4 – Determine the meaning of words and phrases as they are used in a text, including figurative language such as metaphors and similes.	*In May* by William Henry Davies
RL.5.2 – Determine a theme of a story, drama, or poem from details in the text, including how characters in a story or drama respond to challenges or how the speaker in a poem reflects upon a topic	I Wandered Lonely as a Cloud by William Wordsworth

Common Core Language Arts – Writing

W.3.5 – With guidance and support from peers and adults develop and strengthen writing as needed by planning, revising and editing.	*Liberty* by James Whitcomb Riley
W.4.4 – Produce clear and coherent writing in which the development and organization are appropriate to task, purpose, and audience.	*Child and Mother* by Eugene Field
W.5.2.D – Use precise language and domain-specific vocabulary to inform about or explain the topic	*I Wandered Lonely as a Cloud* by William Wordsworth
W.5.3.A – Orient the reader by establishing a situation and introducing a narrator and/or characters; organize an event sequence that unfolds naturally.	*In May* by William Henry Davies

MAY LEARNING STANDARDS
ISTE Technology Standards 2015

ISTE.1 – Creativity and innovation - Students demonstrate creative thinking, construct knowledge and develop innovative products and processes using technology.	Lesson – Mary Cassatt Paintings – Students will work in groups to gather images of Mary Cassatt paintings. They will use their favorites in a multimedia presentation. After viewing the presentations, they will paint a watercolor using her art as a model.
ISTE.2 – Communication and collaboration – Students used digital media and environments to communicate and work collaboratively, including at a distance, to support individual learning and contribute to the learning of others.	Lesson – Writing a Thank You Letter to a Service Member or Veteran –Students work collaboratively to interact with groups that communicate with veterans to learn how to send letters and recordings of thanks.
ISTE.3 – Research and information fluency – Students apply digital tools to gather, evaluate and use information.	Lesson – Mother Goose Day – Students find and listen to Mother Goose nursery rhymes on the Internet and use a variety several digital tools to present original rhymes of their own.
ISTE.4 – Critical thinking, problem solving and decision making – Students use critical thinking skills to plan and conduct research, manage projects, solve problems, and make informed decisions using appropriate digital tools and resources.	Lesson – Scratch Flowers – Using Scratch, students learn mathematical and computational ideas as they create animations, games, music, art and interactive stories. Students practice the design process as they execute their Scratch projects. They imagine, create, experiment, share, reflect and reimagine. Students start with an idea and build a working prototype. They experiment and debug to tweak their projects to the desired results

NGSS and ETS1 Science and Engineering Standards 2015

3-5-ETS1-1. – Define a simple design problem reflecting a need or a want that includes specified criteria for success and constraints on materials, time, or cost.	Maypole Constructions – Students assume the work of construction engineers with the task of building a maypole. They survey the grounds for an ideal spot to place the maypole and build scale models. They make sketches, diagrams and plot plans as they build their models and prepare and present proposals.
3-5-ETS1-2. – Generate and compare multiple possible solutions to a problem based on how well each is likely to meet the criteria and constraints of the problem.	Squishy Circuits – In this lesson, student engineers work in four groups and become circuit designers. They will use two different kinds of homemade play dough to demonstrate electrical properties by lighting up LEDs and spinning motors.
3-5-ETS1-3. – Plan and carry out fair tests in which variables are controlled and failure points are considered to identify aspects of a model or prototype that can be improved.	Product Engineers – Working as product engineers, student groups will design and manufacture perfumes made from wildflowers. They will perform a preliminary fragrance test of many wildflowers and select one to produce in quantity. Students will "manufacture" a number of sample vials with labels for classmates to try.
NGSS MS-ETS1-2 – Evaluate completing design solutions using a systematic process to determine how well they meet the material and constraints of the problem.	Pop-Up Cards – Students learn the mechanics of creating simple pop-up cards. After sharing their first designs, students explore more complicated patterns and examples on the web. Their subsequent designs will be more intricate with further tinkering.

About Us

GARY CARNOW has been a classroom teacher, administrator, author and educational consultant. Dr. Carnow specializes in administrative and instructional technologies, grants and funding procurement, instructional program development, emerging technologies, makerspaces and 3D printing. He has consulted for major hardware and software computer companies and has written extensively for Tech&Learning magazine. He was one of the first educators to provide content for AOL and the Scholastic Network. Beverly and Gary have written educational materials together for over twenty-five years.

BEVERLY ELLMAN is an educator who has enjoyed wearing many different hats. She has been a classroom teacher, an author of educational publications and an educational product developer. She has co-taught several classes which combined poetry and multimedia through UCLA extension with Joyce Koff. In addition, Joyce and Beverly have worked together presenting educational workshops to various elementary and middle school teachers. She has enjoyed watching the enthusiasm, energy, and creativity sparked in students as they experience learning and master STEM content.

JOYCE KOFF is a poet and a teacher. Her work has been published in numerous poetry journals and she has taught in elementary and middle schools in her self-created program. Joyce makes the reading, understanding and writing of poetry accessible to all students and these methods are applied in this book. Joyce has also conducted classes at UCLA demonstrating to teachers how valuable and rewarding the teaching of hands-on poetry can be. As the resident poet at Coeur d'Alene Elementary School in Venice, California, she taught poetry for over 25 years and was part of the art's team that was awarded the prestigious Los Angeles Music Center's Bravo Award. Joyce lives in Los Angeles with her husband.

SIAN BOWMAN has never lost the giddy excitement she experienced as child when drawing and painting. After graduating from Aberystwyth University with a Masters in Fine Art, specializing in children's book illustration, she started freelancing as an illustrator. She is in her element working on picture books and educational books for children. She finds inspiration for her characters in walking her wonderful, cheeky whippet, Jet, through the countryside of Mid Wales - where her imagination can wander. You can learn more about Sian at sianbowman.com.

202